RAF HAWKINGE
IN OLD PHOTOGRAPHS

RAF HAWKINGE
IN OLD PHOTOGRAPHS

COLLECTED BY
ROY HUMPHREYS

ALAN SUTTON

Alan Sutton Publishing Limited
Phoenix Mill · Far Thrupp · Stroud · Gloucestershire

First Published 1991

British Library Cataloguing in Publication Data

RAF Hawkinge in old photographs.
I. Title   II. Humphreys, Roy S.
358.4170942

ISBN 0-86299-938-3

Typeset in 9/10 Korinna.
Typesetting and origination by
Alan Sutton Publishing Limited.
Printed in Great Britain by
The Bath Press, Avon.

CONTENTS

INTRODUCTION

With the passage of time an effective curtain was drawn over the history of RAF Hawkinge – until 1990 when it was suddenly draw aside to reveal, during the fiftieth anniversary of the Battle of Britain, that RAF Hawkinge, not surprisingly, was just as important as the decisive battle fought in the skies above Kent. A view often expressed by those old enough to have experienced the last war is that to have lost *that* particular battle would have proved catastrophic and the beginning of a new Dark Age.

I believe it would be quite wrong if the story of this once famous front line airfield was to remain a closed book to those people anxious to learn of its colourful history. But to describe its many remarkable activities in a few words is no simple task, so intense and varied was its role. This book of old photographs attempts to offer a few preliminary brush strokes.

RAF Hawkinge finally closed down in December 1961. Its closure marked the end of fifty-four years of aviation history. The pomp and ceremony marking such a sad occasion – the guard of honour, the two bands, one RAF, the other WAAF, the hauling down of the RAF ensign for the last time, and the speeches – pursued its inevitable course. When the last bugle note of the Last Post faded into the distance the station ceased to exist.

Since then the old aerodrome has seen many changes. The once proud and immaculate buildings gradually deteriorated into a state of decay and dilapidation, while more than half of the grass airfield, surrounded by broken fences and a cracked perimeter track, returned to farmland where cattle and sheep grazed and wheat crops flourished in the summer sunshine.

More recently the old buildings of the original camp site have been replaced with a new housing estate. While the officers' mess stands forlornly in a state of limbo, the charred rafters of the west wing pointing grotesquely towards the sky, golden corn ripens where frenetic pilots once took off to do battle.

The aerodrome came into being before the First World War, when a Dutch aviator rented a couple of small fields just west of the village of Uphill (now Hawkinge). He designed and built an experimental flying machine of welded tube, covered with mutton cloth and tied together with miles of stranded wire. W.B. Megone never flew his machine, however, giving that dubious task to a friend, Victor Russell, who bounced all over the little field in frantic delight like a demented kangaroo.

Had it not been for the Dutchman's pioneer efforts, however, the field might never have been selected in 1915 by the Royal Flying Corps for a landing ground.

Such modest beginnings were typical of most early aerodromes, and the Barnhouse Flying Field, as it was then called, with three Bessoneau canvas hangars *in situ*, provided maintenance and refuelling facilities for aircraft *en route* to France. When more permanent buildings were being erected in 1917 the aerodrome officially became the Aerodrome Despatch Section Hawkinge.

The pungent aroma of castor oil, and the sound of whirring propellers and spluttering engines, brought a new fascination to the village. Those early sounds and signs of military aviation were to last for over four decades, during which time aircraft design and military air power altered considerably and, through strategic locality, the aerodrome became a vital link in our defence system.

In the post-War resettlement period the RAF front line strength of over 3,000 aircraft withered, by the dawn of the new decade, to just a few squadrons. But defence of the realm was still an important consideration and, in recognition of that and our overseas commitments, a Home Defence Air Force was envisaged.

This brought to Hawkinge its first fighter squadron. Commanded by Sqn. Ldr. Sir Norman Leslie, No. 25 Squadron assembled the Sopwith Snipe fighters which were soon flying over Folkestone and the surrounding area. During a short break, when the squadron left for Turkey where they were involved in the Chanak crisis, two other fighter squadrons had re-formed at Hawkinge. By 1927 No. 25 Squadron had returned, and in the succeeding years, the most colourful period in RAF history, squadron aircraft were daubed with unit insignia.

When new aircraft designs were introduced No. 25 Squadron changed their Snipes for the Gloster Grebe of the mid-1920s. Then came the ponderous Armstrong Whitworth Siskin. The Siskin was replaced in the early 1930s by the Sidney Camm-designed Hawker Fury Interceptor, later updated by the Super Fury.

It is the era of the Furys that is especially remembered for the magnificent synchronized formation flying techniques. Individual flying expertise was the result of peace-time training, and the tranquillity of meadow and country lane was often shattered by high-powered aero engines, long before the Luftwaffe entered our skies. The officers' mess ante-room displayed a variety of silver cups and trophies in recognition of the squadron's professionalism.

The incomparable Fury gave way to the Hawker Demon two-seater fighter, then came the Gloster Gladiator and finally the Bristol Blenheim. It was the Blenheim which caused No. 25 Squadron to move from Hawkinge. The medium-bomber was unsuited to operate from a grass airfield.

They left behind No. 2 Army Co-operation Squadron who had shared airfield facilities since 1935. Initially the A.C. Squadron had been equipped with the Hawker Audax two-seater aircraft, but these were changed for the Hawker Hector, to be replaced by the Westland Lysander.

By 1936 the defence structure had been completely reorganized and Fighter Command was born with a multiple Group system, each Group responsible for its own particular area. No. 11 Group covered the south-east of England. Within each Group were the Sector Stations, whose operational status would control fighter squadrons in any given area of defence. Of the seven Sector Stations in No. 11 Group only one, Biggin Hill, was in Kent. Sector Stations were long-established, and comprised full repair, maintenance, medical and HQ facilities. More importantly perhaps, they used a number of forward 'satellite' aerodromes from which the fighter squadrons could operate.

RAF Hawkinge was one of these satellite aerodromes, where fighters would refuel and re-arm and then wait on 'advanced readiness'.

The new structure was a considerable improvement on the old defence concepts of the 1920s, providing a well organized and clearly defined operational chain of command. But the provision of fighters, strategically placed on coastal aerodromes, without an early warning system was inadequate.

Before 1938 there was heavy reliance upon an established acoustic warning system manned, for the most part, by the Territorial Army, who trained with odd-looking mechanical gadgetry not wholly reliable in all circumstances. By mid-1938, however, the development of Radar-Location had advanced sufficiently to enable our fighter squadrons, many still equipped with obsolete biplanes, to meet opposing forces with a degree of success never before possible.

Peace-time flying became a memory when, in 1939, Great Britain declared war on Germany. Almost overnight, it seemed, the silver-doped biplanes of yesteryear were gone. Pilots were now part of a new adventure. They still represented an élite force, but many were wondering whether the training had provided them with enough confidence.

Aerodrome defence became all important. The Inspector-General and his entourage of Army officers arrived to advise on such matters as where to site the machine-guns, trenches and dug-outs, light ack-ack guns and thousands of sandbags. Blast-pens for aircraft and camouflaged buildings quickly put the aerodrome on a war footing.

From out of snow-laden skies came the first eight-gun fighters of No. 3 Squadron, who began operating their Channel patrols in the first snows of winter. Hawkinge was almost ready for a war which drew closer to England with every passing hour.

But someone, somewhere, thought differently. The Hurricanes of No. 3 Squadron left, and in their place came hundreds of young airmen to join a newly formed Recruiting Pool.

Probably even more bizarre was the sudden arrival of a Queen Mary trailer loaded with crates containing dismantled aircraft and equipment of No. 1 Pilotless Aircraft Unit. When the weather improved a couple of boffins from the Royal Aircraft Establishment at Farnborough erected aerial pylons and wireless apparatus, and flew Queen Wasp pilotless aircraft around the area.

No. 2 (A.C.) Squadron had already moved to France. Their place was taken by No. 16 (A.C.) Squadron who moved over from Lympne. They began their daily routine by providing targets for the gunners in their sandbagged emplacements. The boffins wondered if they, in any way, contributed to Field Marshal Goering's confusion.

During the Dunkirk evacuation of the BEF in May and June 1940, a special briefing room was established in the Haskard Target building, originally built for No. 2 (A.C.) Squadron in 1934. No. 22 (A.C.) Group was responsible for supplying our beleaguered troops at Calais. Air Vice Marshal Blount was in command of the unit called 'Back Component', which dealt with the many complexities of the evacuation as the German Army rapidly advanced. Blenheims flew out of Hawkinge with fighter escort to attack enemy positions.

Then, in July 1940, the Battle of Britain began. Hawkinge was to become famous and prove invaluable to our defence system. When Luftwaffe activity increased over south-east England the Hurricanes and Spitfires increased their daily sorties between dawn and dusk.

Aerial battles, at anything from 2,000 to 20,000 ft, were commonplace in that hot summer. Many exploits of individual gallantry are now legends in the annals of historical documents. The Battle of Britain was the last period in British history in which close aerial combat between two élite air forces was witnessed.

Hawkinge became a front line base for refuelling and re-arming fighters of many types – before, during and after the heat of battle. Visiting fighters used the airfield as a jump-off point to attack the raiding German formations of bombers and their fighter escorts. Later, Hawkinge received its own resident squadron of fighters and engaged the enemy over land and sea and, using its proximity to France, attacked the enemy over his own territory.

RAF Hawkinge continued to fight right through the Second World War to the end of hostilities in 1945. Almost every kind of duty, both in peace and war, will be found within these pages. These duties include the normal peace-time training programmes – the weekly battle climbs, aerobatics and displays – then, with the outbreak of the Second World War, came the fighter patrols of the Battle of Britain period, the reconnaissance patrols, the air sea rescue patrols and, last but by no means least, the bomber escort sorties.

As a front line aerodrome throughout the last war, Hawkinge saw action unfold day by day and knew the pain and suffering caused by minor accidents, enemy action and sheer disaster. Many airmen were decorated for valour and heroism; and many more died flying from its green field in our hour of need.

When the airfield closed in 1945 Sqn. Ldr. J. Littler wrote in the station diary, 'RAF Hawkinge, which has, since the outbreak of hostilities, played so very important a part in the defence of Great Britain and the Empire, is closing down to a Care and Maintenance basis. At no period during the six years of war has the station been non-operational. It can only be hoped that the Air Council in their wisdom will find it possible to use once more an RAF Station that has achieved immortal fame and earned the gratitude of mankind in general.'

The words Care and Maintenance were like a sentence of death. Nevertheless, the Air Council did re-open Hawkinge on 1 June 1947 as the WAAF Depot in No. 22 Group, Technical Training Command. In the following year it became an Officer Course Training Unit and, when the WAAF were re-designated WRAF, the depot remained there until the final closure in December 1961.

Many of the old buildings remaining today serve as a vast memorial to the freedom that was once won here. Sometimes, if you listen hard enough, you can still hear roaring aircraft engines, bomb explosions, the staccato sound of machine-guns, the boom of cannon and the wail of sirens. Memories lurk in every corner. History was made here – at the dispersals, in the little wooden flying control room, out on the perimeter track and in the tiny mortuary.

Fighter squadrons would no longer arrive to be cared for, their aircraft fussed over, the young pilots revered and respected. No more would the Tannoy blare out the word 'scramble', nor the mess corridors echo with the boisterous babbling of youthful voices. Gone were the days of frenetic scrambles, nervous tension and soiled cockpits. Gone also the cheerful competition of 'kills' and the sadness of lost friends.

In 1990, the fiftieth anniversary of the Battle of Britain, it was perhaps fitting, that there should be a fight to save the old aerodrome from the developer's bulldozer. Everyone who has shared in the reward of that particular victory in the summer of

1940 should perhaps feel a little ashamed if this last untouched operational front line fighter station is allowed to quietly succumb to the whim of a developer. These old photographs will underline the importance of retaining this historical site, and preserving it as a memorial to England's 'Finest Hour'.

Roy Humphreys
Hawkinge 1990

SECTION ONE

1915–1919

THE 'MAYFLY' PUSHER BIPLANE designed by W.B. Megone, a Dutch pioneer aviator, was built at the Barnhouse flying ground, Hawkinge in 1912. It was the first flying machine seen at Hawkinge and was built of spruce and welded metal tube covered with mutton cloth.

VICTOR HUNT poses with the home-made 10 ft propeller of Megone's flying machine at the door of the hangar. The propeller was driven by a 60hp Green engine connected through a Hele-Shaw clutch and was often reshaped with a spokeshave. Megone was reluctant to pilot his experimental flying machine and bestowed that dubious honour upon Victor, who fearlessly tackled the job with true pioneer spirit.

THIS IS THE ONLY KNOWN PHOTOGRAPH OF MEGONE'S FIRST DESIGN which used the King-post method of wing bracing. As you will see, the wing area was a primitive sesquiplane. The 'Mayfly' was considered to be an unsophisticated, ugly and grossly overweight contraption.

THE FINAL DESIGN OF THE 'MAYFLY', photographed here by Megone himself, shows the inter-wing struts which gave added strength to the cumbersome wing area. There were few standards upon which Megone could base his ideas and, although other pioneers had been successful, much was beyond Megone's comprehension.

THE EARLIEST KNOWN PHOTOGRAPH OF THE ROYAL FLYING CORPS AEROPLANE DESPATCH SECTION, Hawkinge, taken in 1916. The hangar built by the Dutchman Megone can be seen on the right and was used by the RFC until late 1917. Also in the picture are BE2cs and an FE2b, ready for their delivery flight to squadrons serving at the Western Front, France.

THE PRIMITIVE MEDICAL INSPECTION ROOM at Hawkinge was used by Dr Stephen Pritchard in 1919, when he was medical officer to No. 120 Squadron who were based at the aerodrome, flying mail to the continent. The wooden building remained in use until 1924, when a more permanent structure was erected.

THE ROYAL FLYING CORPS PERSONNEL who were the first to arrive at the Barnhouse flying ground in September 1915. Within just a few weeks they had erected three Bessoneau canvas hangars and had extended the flying area by removing hedges and trees. The first military aeroplanes to use the new airfield were the BE2cs of No. 12 Squadron, who were *en route* to St Omer in France.

THE SKELETAL REMAINS OF A BESSONEAU HANGAR damaged in a freak storm. Bereft of their protective canvas which had been blown over 200 yd away, several flying machines have been severely damaged. Villagers had often ridiculed the RFC. They knew only too well how the high winds blustered across the North Downs with fearsome results.

LIEUTENANT DONALD W. CLAPPEN, photographed here outside the original Megone hangar, was a ferry pilot with the RFC in 1916. With only a canvas belt round their waist, ferry pilots were not encouraged to show off. There were no shoulder straps or parachute and if a young pilot decided to perform a stunt or two it was generally hoped the centrifugal force would keep him glued to his seat.

THIS SOPWITH SNIPE 7F1 (F2346) was one of a batch of 200 built before the Armistice in November 1918. It was seen at Hawkinge when the canvas hangars were still being used near the western boundary, although by that time the programme of rebuilding on a permanent level was well established.

THIS PHOTOGRAPH CLEARLY SHOWS how the airfield looked in 1917 during the days when aircraft were being flown to France almost daily. In the picture are SE5s and Avro 504s. The famous SE5 was a sturdy little aeroplane coming off the production lines at the Royal Aircraft Establishment in the spring of 1917, and by the autumn of that year it proved a formidable opponent.

A SOPWITH 5F1 DOLPHIN, seen at Hawkinge in 1918. Purists will probably argue about whether it was originally destined for No. 23 Squadron. The white triangle on the fuselage was later replaced at squadron level with a white circle. Even more confusing is the J9 stencilled on the rudder and the J6 on the fuselage. Which lettering is correct is neither here nor there, for the Dolphin was built in the first batch and came off the production line in October 1918.

PURCHASES OF FRENCH AIRCRAFT by GHQ, British Expeditionary Force in 1917 helped to equip and maintain a number of RFC squadrons. This French Nieuport 27 V-strutter arrived at Hawkinge that same year and, although the serial number is not clear, it still carries the French roundel.

IT WAS A THREE POINT LANDING WITH A DIFFERENCE for this Avro 504 when it overturned in a nearby field in 1918. The black triangle denotes No. 2 Squadron. Broken propeller blades often turned up in local houses with either a clock or a barometer inserted into the blade.

ONE OF SEVERAL HANDLEY PAGE 0/400s sent to Hawkinge in 1918 stands in front of both No. 5 and No. 6 hangars, which were purpose-built to house the HP four-engined biplane V/1500, destined to bomb Germany. The 0/400 was one of several which arrived at the aerodrome and this particular machine was used during the 1921 air display. Many 0/400s were broken up at Hawkinge and pieces of fuselage were used by local farmers as chicken coops.

THIS SPAD S7, almost certainly another purchase from the French, was coloured dark green with yellow wheel discs. S7s helped to equip No. 19 and No. 23 Squadrons but it is not known to which unit this particular Spad belonged when it appeared at Hawkinge in 1917.

THIS BRISTOL FIGHTER limped in to Hawkinge in 1918 when it developed engine trouble. It was based at the No. 1 School of Aerial Gunnery, the Redoubt, Dymchurch. The School of Aerial Gunnery moved to New Romney in November 1918.

THIS DH9 WAS ONE OF SEVERAL operated by No. 120 Squadron during their mail carrying
service from Hawkinge to France. It was photographed by Dr Stephen Pritchard in 1919.
Mail destined for the Army of Occupation in Germany was originally flown to Maisoncelle,
France, but later flights were made to Cologne.

ROYAL AIR FORCE.

AERIAL POST.

TO BE CARRIED BY THE PILOT OF A POSTAL AEROPLANE

Extract from G.R.O. No. 819, dated 23rd January, 1919 :—

"6104 AERIAL POST. In the course of long flights undertaken in connection with the Aerial Post, pilots are frequently forced to land, on account of weather conditions or engine failure, etc.

In such cases, pilots have been instructed to apply to the nearest unit, who will make every endeavour to provide transport to convey the mails to the nearest Military post office, with the least possible delay.

(254 (Q.A.); 23-1-19)."

Name of Pilot A. F. HORDERN AFC (capt)

Squadron 120ᵗʰ AERIAL MAIL

Location of Squadron HAWKINGE

THE FIRST MAIL RUN FROM THE UNITED KINGDOM was flown on 1 March 1919, when four DH9s took off from Hawkinge with twenty-three mail bags. The mail was prepared by the Royal Engineers Postal Section, based in Folkestone, and each pilot carried an identification card.

HAWKINGE IN THE GRIP OF WINTER was photographed from a low flying DH9 in February 1919 by Dr Stephen Pritchard, then medical officer to No. 120 Squadron.

THIS DH4, designed as a two-seater day bomber, and seen at Hawkinge in 1919, was pressed into service to carry food and other scarce commodities to the unfortunate Belgians.

AN ACCUMULATION OF COMMISSIONED AND NON-COMMISSIONED RANKS, brought about by dis-
banded squadrons, became a distinct embarrassment for the aerodrome administration. A
high proportion had served in regiments of the line before being drafted into the Royal
Flying Corps. Many were engaged in the speed up of communications between the forces of
occupation and England.

ROYAL ENGINEERS POSTAL SECTION PERSONNEL load up a DH9 with mail bags. Stripped completely, the rear cockpit became a cavernous storage area. Sometimes a passenger who needed to return to his unit in Germany was taken along.

THIS MOTLEY GROUP of No. 120 Squadron pilots, arranged around sacks of flour, was photographed in 1919. Under the aegis of Aircraft Transport & Travel Ltd, they were happily engaged flying urgent supplies to Belgium.

THE ORIGINAL OFFICERS' MESS, seen here on the right with the glass porch (compare p. 45), was constructed during the First World War period. The building on the left was the officer accommodation, used during the Second World War as an Headquarters containing administration offices. The HQ survived the air raids of 1940, but the officers' mess was hit by bombs and demolished.

SECTION TWO

1920–1929

Price SIXPENCE.

Aerial Training Display

by

No. 25 Squadron,
Royal Air Force,

at

Hawkinge Aerodrome,

on

Wednesday, 3rd August,

At 3 p.m.

1921

Printed by F. J. Parsons, Ltd., "Herald" Works, The Bayle, Folkestone.

THE FIRST AIR DISPLAY, officially called the RAF Tournament, was held at RAF Hendon on 3 July 1920. No. 25 (F) Squadron, then based at RAF Hawkinge, attended the display which was a resounding success. On 3 August 1921 RAF Hawkinge put on their own show which was the first of its kind at the aerodrome.

THIS DELIGHTFUL WATERCOLOUR PAINTING of a Sopwith Snipe 7F1 in No. 25 Squadron livery – two black bars in sinister – was painted by Brian C. Sherren in 1922. A schoolboy at the time, he later drew aircraft illustrations for manufacturers that were published in aviation magazines.

UNDOUBTEDLY THE BIGGEST PROJECTS BUILT during the First World War were No. 5 and No. 6 hangars, originally intended to house the Handley Page 0/400s and the larger HP V/1500s. An unusual feature included the construction of culverts beneath the floors to accommodate bombs. No. 6 hangar was pulled down before the last war, but No. 5 hangar was demolished by the Luftwaffe in 1940.

THE FIRST FIGHTERS TO USE HAWKINGE IN A PEACE-TIME ROLE belonged to No. 25 squadron, who mobilized on 26 April 1920. The Sopwith Snipe 7F1 was clearly a development of the famous Sopwith Camel Scout. Powered by the Bentley aero-engine the squadron's Snipes were, at one time, the only fighters to defend the United Kingdom.

NO. 25 SQUADRON LEFT ENGLAND FOR TURKEY in October 1922, where they were involved in the Channak crisis for a period of only six months. On their return in 1923 they re-assembled their Snipes from the packing cases and were, once again, soon engaged in defence strategy over the English Channel.

THIS SINGLE-SEATER SPORTING BIPLANE, called 'Little Whippet', was made by Austins in 1919. Designed by J.W. Kenworthy, it was powered by a 45hp six-cylinder Anzani radial engine (cost £275) and had folding wings. It was photographed at Hawkinge when the aircraft arrived for assessment trials in 1924. An Avro 504 belonging to No. 17 squadron can be seen in the hangar.

FLYING OFFICER D.A. BOYLE, later Marshal of the Royal Air Force, Sir Dermot A. Boyle GCB, KBE, KCVO, AFC, is on the left of this trio photographed in front of the Snipe of 'A' Flight, No. 17 Squadron at Hawkinge in 1925. With him are Sqn. Ldr. Don (middle) and FO H.R.D. Waghorn (on the right). Waghorn won the 1929 Schneider Trophy contest.

'A' FLIGHT PERSONNEL OF NO. 17 SQUADRON photographed at Hawkinge in 1925. The squadron re-formed there on 1 April 1924, and received the Sopwith Snipe 7F1 as their first mount.

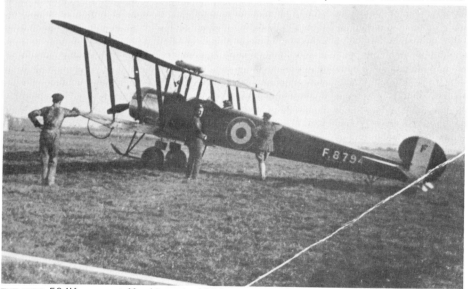

THE AVRO 504K, seen at Hawkinge in 1924, was one of two built by Parnell & Sons and allotted to No. 25 Squadron for training purposes. This type of aeroplane was the first to be delivered to the RFC, as early as 1912, and variants were still in service in the late 1930s.

NO. 17 SQUADRON HAD BEGUN TO TAKE SHAPE under the eagle eye of Sqn. Ldr. J. Leacroft MC by late May 1924 after receiving their Sopwith Snipes in crates which were unloaded from wagons at Folkestone Junction railway station. The unit insignia was only slightly less dismal than that of their companions in 25 Squadron. The only difference was that the two black lines ran in pointed waves and in parallel.

NO. 17 SQUADRON CHANGED THEIR SNIPES for the Hawker Woodcock in March 1926. Some of these were fitted with full night-flying equipment, and it was on a nightly excursion that Sgt. Tompkins came to a sticky end. He bent his Woodcock whilst making a landing in fog and received a broken shoulder blade for his trouble.

NO. 25 SQUADRON became the first fighter unit to receive the newly-designed Gloster Grebe, in October 1924. This was the first machine of twelve in the batch assembled at the aerodrome, and was photographed by an airman immediately after it made its first test flight. The Grebe, however, developed an alarming wing flutter when diving and was the cause of many crashes until the fault was cured.

AS EACH GREBE WAS ASSEMBLED they were test flown, and when everyone was satisfied with the performance, they were given the squadron insignia. In this line-up of Grebes the three on the extreme right have received their two black lines in sinister, while those on the left await the attention of black dope and paint brush.

DURING AIR-TO-GROUND FIRING EXERCISES on 9 December 1926, when the Grebes had been diving towards their target, a series of circles cut into the turf near the centre of the airfield, FO Purvis lost control of his machine. It dived into a hollow near Terlingham Manor Farm. Purvis, a nephew of Sir John Gilmour, then Secretary of State for Scotland, died instantly.

A FEATURE OF PEACE-TIME TRAINING was the weekly battle flight made at squadron strength. On other occasions they joined in with other fighter and bomber units in air exercises which covered the whole of the British Isles. Sqn. Ldr. A.H. Peck DSO, MC, known as 'Bushel', stands on the extreme right with his No. 25 Squadron pilots at Odinham, Kent in 1926.

THIS UNUSUAL PHOTOGRAPH taken inside No. 2 hangar at Hawkinge was sent to me by Air Commodore W.K. Beisiegel. Beneath each Jaguar engine is a drip tray. The photograph also shows the wooden bow-strut construction of the Belfast hangar, and the massive iron doors that opened on rollers and guide-rails. The white-painted brick pillars divided the hangar into either two or three separate bays.

ANOTHER PHOTOGRAPH FROM W.K. BEISIEGEL, taken in 1928, shows his Gloster Grebe II J7569 having its engine run up. Beisiegel was destined to play cricket for the RAF and often flew to matches in his Grebe. Charles Beamish, the third of four very famous brothers, also made use of service aircraft to attend the Irish Rugby season.

PASSING OUT FROM RAF CRANWELL, young pilots were usually sent to the squadron where their special abilities would be of most service. Their subsequent arrival and initiation at squadron level was a somewhat emotional experience. Flt. Lt. 'Revver' Ford, later Group Captain R.J.A. Ford CBE, remembered discomfort when diving from 10,000 ft. The medical officer advised him to pinch his nose and blow hard. He left the surgery wondering how he could manage that and dive at full throttle — stick in one hand and nose in the other.

SQN. LDR. W.H. 'PORKY' PARK, CO of No. 25 Squadron in 1927, was a great personality at RAF Hawkinge. Unfortunately he died the following year after an emergency operation at the Folkestone Victoria Hospital. Park is remembered for his strict discipline, coupled with a gentlemanly benevolence.

THE GLOSTER GREBE, powered by the Armstrong Siddely Jaguar radial engine, possessed a top speed of nearly 150 m.p.h. Although it was one of the most pleasing biplane fighters of that era, often called 'the little fighter with the big heart,' it had developed wing flutter. Nevertheless, as a direct result of its popularity there was every justification for modifying the wing area, thus extending its useful life.

FLIGHT COMMANDER W.E. SWANN (standing far left in this picture) succeeded Sqn. Ldr. Park when he fell ill. His first duty was to take No. 25 Squadron to RAF Hendon to give a display to the Sultan of Muscat and Oman. Flt. Lt. R.J.A. Ford is seated on the right outside the bell tent.

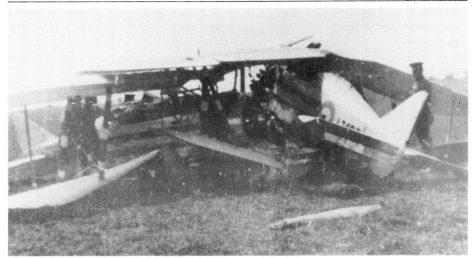

SINCE THE FITTING OF V-STRUTS to the Grebes in 1926 there had been few accidents. However, in February 1928, two Grebes collided in mid-air and in poor visibility. PO Walsh, who had previously been involved in a mid-field collision, managed to parachute to safety, but Flt. Lt. Watson spun to the ground with his machine. Here we see the tangled remains of the two Grebes following the earlier incident. Both Walsh and Flt. Lt. Ford escaped injury.

FLT. LT. 'REVVER' FORD stands on the outer wing, on a special platform, ready to take a parachute jump from a Vickers Vimy. When the Vimy had reached the allotted height the parachutist was given a signal by the pilot to swing round the wing strut; another signal and the 'chute was released from its pack. When the 'chute was fully extended the parachutist would jump backwards to clear the trailing edge of the wing.

THE VICKERS VIMY, coloured white overall, and used for parachute training at Hawkinge, had been salvaged from the Wessex Storage Unit, which was based at the aerodrome, where old aircraft were broken up and sold. There were plenty of spare parts to keep the Vimy flying for many years.

A DH9 BEING DELIVERED TO THE WESSEX STORAGE UNIT arrived in spectacular fashion in 1929, when the pilot decided to make his landing approach between two hay-ricks. A hot engine and spilled petrol set the hay-ricks alight but the pilot was dragged from the wreckage with only a few scratches to show for his ignominious landing.

THE MID-AIR COLLISION OF TWO GREBES (see p. 38) resulted in J7412 crashing into a house on the outskirts of the village. It was fortunate that PO Walsh had baled out. Sir Samuel Hoare, then Air Minister, had stated in the House of Commons in answer to a question on air accidents that the RAF had not yet discovered a remedy against flying accidents.

PO BEISEIGEL STANDS ON THE RIGHT, hands on hips, and waits patiently for his Grebe to be put back on an even keel after it overturned when landing in a strong cross wind. Sir Samuel Hoare took the opportunity to inform the House that every possible precaution was being taken, and further, that the standard of training, inspection and supervision of aircraft and airmen, was the highest in the world.

NO. 25 SQUADRON took delivery of the Armstrong Whitworth Siskin in July 1929. The Siskin was the first service fighter to use an all metal construction with fabric covering. Powered by a 450hp Siddely Jaguar engine, the aircraft was too large, heavy and docile, with a rather disappointing performance. The Siskin did not live up to the manufacturer's claim of 156 m.p.h. at sea level.

ESPECIALLY SUITABLE FOR DAY AND NIGHT OPERATIONS, the Siskin was fitted with flame-damping exhaust stacks, as well as wireless and small bomb racks, full night-flying equipment and cockpit heating. This latter inovation was beneficial but also a potential killer. Sgt. Pearce lost his life in this crash on Folkestone sports field after he had succumbed to carbon monoxide fumes emitted by the heater system.

THE SISKIN WAS A SESQUIPLANE, having a high upper wing with a rather short lower wing. 'Dropping a wing' or 'putting a wing in' were two terms often used in Siskin squadrons following accidents due to the ineffective lower wing-plane. Unofficial manoeuvres, such as this one caused by a strong cross wind, gave tarmac critics much pleasure.

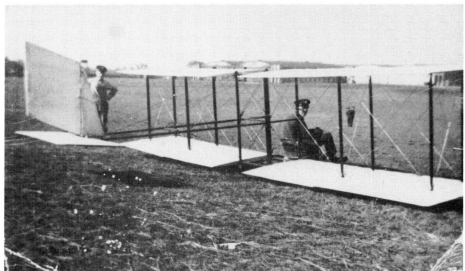

CORPORAL W.B. MANUEL OF NO. 25 SQUADRON sits in the tiny wooden seat of the Octave Chanute glider, which he planned and built at Hawkinge in 1929. He made frequent visits to the London Science Museum, jotting down all the relevant information; back at the aerodrome he spent many months making his replica. On Sundays, when the CO was away, a service aeroplane was often used to tow it into the air.

THIS FOKKER VII A of the Dutch KLM Airline had only just taken off from nearby Lympne, *en route* to Holland, when it developed engine trouble. It made an emergency landing with a dozen passengers at Hawkinge in 1928. Incidentally, this particular passenger liner was later destroyed at Schipol Airport by German bombs on 10 May 1940.

SQUADRON PHOTOGRAPHS were always a feature of service life and there was often little excuse needed to ring up the local photographer for yet another sitting. This particular print was found in the Chadwell album and looks as if it might have been taken in around 1929.

NON-COMMISSIONED OFFICERS were the backbone of the service, as indeed they were in the Army and Navy, and almost certainly still are in today's services. No. 25 Squadron's NCOs pose in 1929 outside the Sergeants' Mess which, incidentally, was bombed in 1940.

DURING SQN. LDR. PROBYN'S STAY AT HAWKINGE the Channel Gliding Club was born. As interest increased in gliding, techniques and design came to occupy the minds of airmen and civilians alike. But serious design inaccuracies had resulted in some hair-raising attempts to get them to fly. Shown here, from left to right, are BAC IV, a Zogling and a Crested Wren.

SECTION THREE

1930–1939

PILOTS OF NO. 25 SQUADRON pose for the photographer on the steps of the old officers' mess in 1932. Back row, left to right: FOs L.F. Brown, A.E. Clouston, T.A. Head, R.G. Harman, R.G. Arnold and PO T.A. Hunter. Middle row: FOs H. St G. Burke, R.P. Garnons-Williams, G.P. MacDonald, Sqn. Ldr. E.G. Bryant MBE, FO C.R. Hancock DFC, F.P.R. Dunworth, N. Gaunt, J. Nesbit-Dufort. Front row: FO A.E. Douglas-Jones, K.B.B. Cross.

SPORTS DAYS were an annual event for resident squadrons, but on the Empire Air Days additional sporting activities were included on the programme. Officers, NCOs and airmen all made their contribution – even the wives, sweethearts and daughters.

ALTHOUGH TYPICAL of most RAF aerodromes in peace-time, in the 1930s Hawkinge in particular became a magnificent fragrant landscape of well-kept paths, flower beds and shrubs. Perfumed flowers mingled with the pungent aroma of petrol and oil, and the solid-looking, white-washed hangars could be seen quite easily from the air over the French coast.

HOW THEY LIVED. This bedroom, in the old officers' mess building, was photographed by PO 'Pat' Burke of No. 25 Squadron in 1933. In the following year a new building programme began, but the new officers' mess was not completed until 1936.

FLT. LT. L.H. STEWART of No. 25 Squadron had stimulated interest in gliding by writing a letter to the local press. By 1930 there were many visitors to the aerodrome and, with the help of Sqn. Ldr. H.M. 'Daddy' Probyn, squadron CO, the Channel Gliding Club was born. In this photograph, taken in a field opposite the Valiant Sailor public house at Capel le Ferne, are, from left to right: Herr Krause, Susie Lippins, the Master of Sempill, Gordon England, Herr Kronfeld, the manager of the Folkestone Midland Bank, Flt. Lt. L.H. Stewart and Herr Magasuppe.

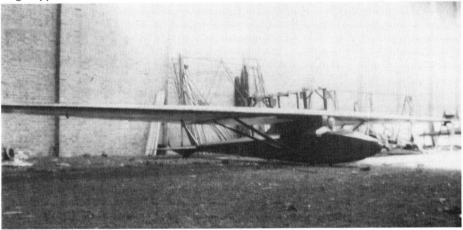

THIS PROFESSOR, seen here in No. 4 hangar, was flown on many occasions by the Belgian glider pilot Miss Susie Lippins. It was later broken by the CO while he was attempting to land. He ended up on a hangar roof. Non-powered flights often took a turn for the worse. Flt. Lt. Fox-Barret was salvaged from the wreckage of one glider that had plummeted to earth from about forty feet.

SQN. LDR. H.M. PROBYN DSO, known throughout the RAF as 'Daddy', was to command the Royal Air Force College at Cranwell during the last war. He was also the proud owner of a Westland Widgeon aeroplane which came fifth in the 1927 King's Cup air race. Newcomers to No. 25 Squadron were sometimes irritated by the Widgeon flying close to their formation. The intrepid CO was actually filming their progress – camera in one hand and control column in the other.

THIS FAIREY FLYCATCHER, seen at the aerodrome in 1930, arrived during one of the Air Defence of Great Britain air exercises. This particular aircraft type was the standard front line fighter of the Fleet Air Arm. Unfortunately there are no unit insignia or serial numbers visible to indicate where it came from.

WAPITI – J9863, flown in this picture by the Marquis of Clydesdale, was CO of No. 602 (City of Glasgow) Auxiliary Squadron. They were on their annual summer camp exercises at Hawkinge in 1931, and both village and station were rudely awakened each morning at first light by the sound of bagpipes.

FLT. LT. HARTRIDGE of No. 504 (County of Nottingham) Squadron, making his landing approach on 7 August 1933, momentarily froze when the Rolls-Royce Condor engine of his Hawker Horsley spluttered and then stopped. Hartridge made a perfect three point landing on the roof of No. 4 hangar. Punctured fuel tanks spilt petrol which ingnited. Pilot and navigator scrambled to safety, but the hangar roof and aircraft in storage were destroyed in the blaze.

THE MOTOR TRANSPORT SECTION OF NO. 25 SQUADRON, displayed here outside No. 1 hangar in 1934, had been cleaned and polished for the CO's weekly inspection. Four years before, Sqn. Ldr. 'Daddy' Probyn used to inspect the camp each week on horseback. He had been a member of the East Kent Hunt.

NO. 25 SQUADRON HAD RECEIVED THE HAWKER FURY INTERCEPTOR FIGHTER, developed from the Sidney Camm-designed Hawker Hornet, by 1932. Powered by the Rolls-Royce Kestrel engine delivering 525hp driving a Watts wooden propeller, it had a top speed of 207 m.p.h. The Fury was fully aerobatic and flew like a dream. It was the envy of many less fortunate fighter squadrons.

THE HAWKINGE FIRE TENDER AND CREW were not often required to exercise their skills, although they had to attend every aircraft crash in the vicinity of the aerodrome. The most serious fire occurred when No. 4 hangar caught alight (see p. 51) and six Blackburn Dart aircraft in storage went up in flames.

SQN. LDR. 'TONY' PAXTON, CO of 25 Squadron in 1934, stands on the left of this picture and is seen briefing his Fury display team for the Hendon Air Display. Left to right: Sqn. Ldr. A. Paxton, Flt. Lt. C.R. Hancock, Sgt. D.A. Upton, Sgt. M. Pearson, Flt. Lt. K.B. Cross, Flt. Lt. Douglas-Jones, FO J.R. Blackburn, Flt. Lt. A.E. Clouston, FO M. Daunt.

THIS 1920S CONCRETE SOUND MIRROR, erected on the downs above the town of Hythe, was one of several early warning sound locators used before the invention of radar. This particular mirror now lays on its face after a landslide during the 1987 storms.

THIS CROSSLEY 30 CWT LORRY AND TRAILER was often in demand during the Air Defence of Great Britain air exercises. This shows the recovery of a No. 3 Squadron Bristol Bulldog fighter which had crashed at Kenardington, Kent in 1934.

SGT. 'MAX' UPTON, one of the most capable and experienced pilots with No. 25 Squadron, had taken this Hawker Hart Trainer up for an engine test. Fog and sea mists obscured the airfield completely when he made his landing attempt, and the Hart received some rough treatment. 'Max' Upton stands on the extreme right of the picture.

NO. 25 SQUADRON FURYS IN BATTLE FORMATION. 'Max' Upton remembered his flight in a Fury: 'She came alive – I could feel the control surfaces functioning beautifully, she only needed a mere touch and she answered perfectly.' On landing he said, 'She settled like a bird – bounded along on her long stroke oleo legs like an ostrich.'

LED BY SQN. LDR. PAXTON, 25 Squadron's Furys, tied together with rubber bungee and flags, put on their display at the 1934 Hendon Air Show. It was a spectacle not to be missed. Each Fury had a length of rubber bungee fixed to the top and bottom of the rear inter-plane strut. Two lengths of stout cord were then tied to the middle of the bungee and the ends were joined by six feet of cord with a breaking strain of only ten pounds. Flags were sewn to the thick cord at intervals.

THE IGNOMINIOUS CRASH OF FLT. LT. NESBITT-DUFORT battered his Fury beyond repair when the engine died on him while taking off for the weekly battle climb. Nesbitt-Dufort flew Lysanders to occupied France during the last war to pick up and deliver 'agents' for the Special Operations Executive.

THIS WHITE-COLOURED DE HAVILAND PUSS MOTH, bearing the black and green triangle of Iraq, was purchased by King Faisal, and arrived at Hawkinge *en route* to the Middle East.

THIS MODEL T FORD HUCKS STARTER was used at Hawkinge for over twenty years to start the engines of the biplane fighters. Demonstrations were given to the general public on Empire Air Days.

THE HAWKINGE WIRELESS SECTION demonstrate their equipment at an Empire Air Day. Members of the public were given an opportunity to send instructions to an aircraft by wireless. Participation in public relations proved costly on one occasion when a Fury pilot was asked to descend closer to the ground than was practicable. The Fury hit the ground at high speed and tipped up on its nose. A very red-faced civilian walked away from the microphone just as the pilot climbed from the cockpit.

SQN. LDR. PAXTON DEMONSTRATES HIS NINE FURY INTERCEPTORS for the benefit of a *Daily Express* photographer. The display sequence of 'tied Furys' followed a certain pattern. Tied together, three flights of three took off in line abreast, turning through 360° to climb to 2,500 ft. They then performed a loop – nine aircraft in V formation – then came a barrel roll and finally the Prince of Wales' Feather, where they broke away in different directions.

THIS AERIAL PHOTOGRAPH was taken in 1930 from a Siskin IIIA of No. 25 Squadron according to the reverse of the original print. The large identification circle shows the letter 'L' which meant that all aircraft approaching the aerodrome would be required to make a left-hand circuit before landing. The series of smaller circles at the bottom of the print was the target for aircraft making an air-to-ground attack.

THE INTERIOR OF THE HASKARD TARGET OR RANGE, which was first introduced at Hawkinge in 1934. Used by the Army Co-operation Squadron, it was originally designed for training in bomb-aiming techniques. A tapestry of fine hessian on rollers had wooded areas, hills, towns and villages, roads and rivers sewn upon it. The raised, glass-covered viewing platform was used by those under instruction. The building was used during the Dunkirk evacuation in 1940, where the HQ called Back Component was set up under Air Vice Marshal C.H.B. Blount.

THIS DH PUSS MOTH, G-ACLW, was owned by Sir Philip Sassoon, then Secretary of State for Air. It was Sir Philip's second private aeroplane and, because it was flown by 'Max' Upton of 25 Squadron, it was a frequent visitor to Hawkinge. Incidentally, G-ACLW is the only aeroplane not to have survived of the four aeroplanes owned by Sir Philip.

THIS DH90 DRAGONFLY was the third aeroplane owned by Sir Philip Sassoon. Sgt. Upton stands beside G-AEDT. 'Max' Upton was often called upon to carry passengers from Port Lympne (Sir Philip's country house) to places such as Paris, Brussels and many aerodromes in this country, such as Croydon, Heston, Hendon and Northolt.

SIR PHILIP SASSOON BT., Secretary of State for Air, MP for Folkestone and Hythe, and honorary Air Commodore of No. 601 (County of London) Auxiliary Squadron, frequently held 'open house' to Hawkinge personnel at his country mansion at Port Lympne.

THIS PERCIVAL Q6, G-AFFD, was the last private aeroplane purchased by Sir Philip Sassoon. This shows the Q6 with 601 Squadron insignia – a winged sword, carried on the fin, and a coiled cobra mounted in front of the windshield. Members of 25 and 2 Squadron used the Q6 for twin engine experience.

A BEAUTIFUL PHOTOGRAPH OF A HAWKER AUDAX of No. 2 (A.C.) Squadron taxiing to position behind the Super Furys of 25 Squadron, for the 1937 affiliation exercises. It was taken by Rex Puttee, an officer in the Territorial Army.

THIS FINE PICTURE OF K1995 illustrates the Message Hook system of retrieving messages from the ground. This particular Audax, of 2 (A.C.) Squadron, was the first production machine, flown on 29 December 1931 by Hawker's chief test pilot, P.E.G. Sayer. K1995 crashed at Hawkinge on 13 August 1936.

HAWKINGE BECAME A STATION HEADQUARTERS in July 1935, under the command of Sqn. Ldr. W.F. Dickson. In November that year No. 2 Army Co-operation Squadron arrived from Manston. Audax K3086 was displayed at the Folkestone Sports Ground, Cheriton Road, for Jubilee Day.

THIS VEGA GULL, G-ACYC, the forerunner of the successful Percival Proctor, was sent to No. 2 (A.C.) Squadron for its 100 hours evaluation trials in 1937. It was used mainly as a squadron taxi.

THIS CIERVA C30A, otherwise known as the Avro 671 Rota I, was originally delivered to the School of Army Co-operation, Odiham. It was photographed during an Air Defence of Great Britain exercise in 1938 at Hawkinge where selected pilots were given instruction on the autogyro.

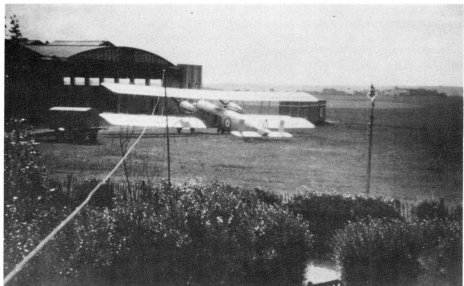

THE VICKERS VALENTIA, seen here standing outside No. 1 hangar in 1936, had arrived for the Empire Air Day display. The photograph was taken by Roy Chadwell, son of the station accountant officer, from the bedroom window of No. 2 O.M.Q. (Officers' Married Quarters).

PILOTS OF 2 SQUADRON POSE FOR THEIR PHOTOGRAPH. On the reverse of the print there are only christian names. From left to right: Ivor, Tony, Jeff, Brian, John, Jimmy and Peter. The last named is Peter Stansfeld, later Group Captain P.W. Stansfeld CBE, DFC.

ANOTHER PICTURE FROM THE CHADWELL ALBUM shows part of the static aircraft on display for the Empire Air Day show. The mounted cavalry in the foreground came from regiments staying at Shorncliffe Camp on their summer exercise.

NO. 25 SQUADRON'S SISKINS fly over the aerodrome in 1931. The photograph was taken by Sqn. Ldr. Probyn, from his privately-owned Westland Widgeon. The 100 ft identification circle cut into the turf and filled with chalk, can still be seen from the air today.

HAWKER AUDAX K3058, of No. 2 (A.C.) Squadron, moves out ready to take off for affiliation exercises with No. 25 Squadron. The function of the Army Co-op squadrons, right up to the Second World War, was to work in close liaison with ground units of infantry, artillery and tanks. Developed from the Hart, the Audax offered an almost unlimited range of variations for all military duties.

FLT. LT. ANDREW GEDDES, later Air Commodore A.J.W. Geddes CBE, DSO, leads three Audax of 'B' Flight, No. 2 Squadron over Loch Ness during a long distance flight in April 1937. Geddes had persuaded Sqn. Ldr. Opie to allow the flight to take place, partly as a photographic exercise, and also to give the pilots long distance flight experience.

HAWKER HECTORS REPLACED THE AUDAX of No. 2 (A.C.) Squadron, and were built by the Westland Aircraft Company at Yeovil under licence. Although the Napier Dagger engine had been on trial since 1933 it was troublesome. The bakelite distributor cap, with its harness of twenty-four leads just behind the propeller boss, was virtually inaccessible and often cracked under extreme heat conditions.

FIGHTER PRODUCTION had made heavy demands on the Rolls-Royce Kestrel engine, and when the new Hector biplane was built the Napier Dagger was chosen to power it. Flt. Lt. Andrew Geddes, who was later to command No. 2 Squadron in France during the 'phoney war' period, is seen here 'daisy-cutting' the Hawkinge turf in his Hector. On 19 May 1940 Geddes, with Leading Aircraftman Clarke as airgunner, attacked a JU87 Stuka over Audenarde, Belgium in Lysander KO-T. The German dive-bomber crashed at Hulsbosch twenty minutes later.

FLT. LT. ANDREW GEDDES with a basin-full of West Highland puppies. When No. 2 Squadron left for Friday Wood, Colchester in February 1937, on an annual camp, they had trouble with their prized goldfish. Over London the gunner, who balanced a glass bowl on his lap, suddenly shouted to Geddes, 'Fish are blowing up like balloons, sir!' Geddes descended to a more reasonable height and the marine life deflated.

THIS SPLENDID PHOTOGRAPH of the patchwork fields around Hawkinge was taken from the rear cockpit of a 2 Squadron Lysander, by LAC David Kirton, facing north and flying at about 15,000 ft. It is not difficult to find RAF Hawkinge. In 1941 the Luftwaffe took a similar reconnaissance shot to show bomb damage sustained at the aerodrome in the 1940 raids (see p. 103).

FORTUNATELY THE STATION WARRANT OFFICER WAS NOWHERE TO BE SEEN when David Kirton (on the left) posed with some of the lads from the 2 Squadron photographic section. The buildings seen in the background still exist. When this photograph was taken Kirton had already applied to become a fighter pilot, a decision which was to cost him his life.

NO. 2 SQUADRON REPLACED THEIR HAWKER HECTORS with the Westland Lysander, affectionately called the 'Lissie', in 1938. A single high-winged monoplane with a fixed undercarriage, it could operate quite easily from small fields. The Lysander was used, during the last war, to carry 'agents' to and from France under the aegis of the SOE. L4697, coded KO-J, prepares to take off for parachute training in 1939.

POINT OF IMPACT WITH MOTHER EARTH. A Leading Aircraftman of No. 2 Squadron, under parachute instruction, nearly collided with a stationery Lysander on the aerodrome. The Irvin parachute was standard equipment for all air crew in the late 1930s.

LAC DAVID KIRTON, a photographer with No. 2 Squadron, took every opportunity to familiarize himself with the cockpit layout of the Lysander. He successfully applied to become a pilot in June 1939, and was subsequently shot down on 8 August 1940, near Manston.

FLT. LT. A.W. GEDDES, in the fore-cockpit, prepares to take his Hector up for a spot of cross-country flying. In this picture the unusual air duct system of the Dagger engine can be seen: two separate ducts sucking in air, one above the other, with the novel 'fish-gill' arrangement at the rear of the engine cowling.

THE PILOTS OF NO. 25 SQUADRON who had been selected to fly in the 1937 display team. From left to right: Sgt. W.T. Jeffery, Sgt. Haine, Sgt. Waley, Flt. Lt. Cameron, Sqn. Ldr. H.H. Down (CO), Flt. Lt. Nedwill, PO Lonsdale, Sgt T. Blackburn and Sgt. Aggett. The Lydd Flight Office board on the hangar wall denoted the air-to-ground firing exercises carried out on the Lydd Ranges. Air-to-ground firing was also undertaken at the Hythe Ranges.

SQN. LDR. H.H. DOWN (see pennant behind cockpit of K7270) leads the nine Fury II's over Herne Bay, Kent in 1937. The first production Fury II (K7263) flew on 3 December 1936, and can be seen here in the middle of this formation. It has often been suggested that if you removed the top wing, put a canopy over the cockpit, replaced the Kestrel with a Merlin and installed a retractable undercarriage you would possess a Hawker Hurricane.

THIS PHOTOGRAPH OF THE FURY IIs IN 'V' FORMATION reminds me of the time when 25 Squadron and 2 Squadron – eighteen aircraft – were on a collision course over Folkestone at little more than 800 ft above sea level. The bar steward remembered it as the day when the greatest quantity of brandy was dispensed in any one day in the officers' mess. The Furys returned to the aerodrome, one by one, after scattering to all points of the compass.

Below, right:
TWO MONTHS AFTER TAKING COMMAND of 25 Squadron, Sqn. Ldr. Donald Fleming was disappointed to hear that his beautiful Fury IIs were to be exchanged for Hawker Demons (shown here). On the preliminary inspection at Catterick he thought the two-seater Demons a sorry-looking lot. There was no comparison with his gleaming Furys standing just a few yards away, looking like fine-tempered blades in a medieval tournament.

THIS WESTLAND LYSANDER L4698 (above) was the second of sixteen delivered to No. 2 (A.C.) Squadron at Hawkinge. Flt. Lt. Geddes is at the controls. Bringing the machine from Yeovil, he could not resist the temptation to stunt it. He threw the 'Lissie' into a loop and did the usual slow roll off the top, but noticed with some annoyance a slight fall-off in flying performance. On inspection after landing it was discovered a brake-slot hinge had broken. Because of this unofficial escapade future Lysanders were modified at the factory.

CAPTAIN PETER STANSFELD, in the uniform of the Royal Tank Corps, but also a Flt. Lt. in No. 2 (A.C.) Squadron, is seen here wearing the 'For Valour' star and ribbon, presented to him by Wing Commander 'Bobby' George (station CO) after Stansfeld had successfully delivered the first Lysander to the squadron from Yeovil.

WING COMMANDER 'BOBBY' GEORGE, station CO, had laid on a reception committee for the arrival of the first Lysander for 2 Squadron. Wg/Cdr. George, who was later Governor of New South Wales, Australia, stands on the left of this trio; in the middle is Sqn. Ldr. W.A. Opie, sqn CO, and on the right is Captain Stansfeld.

THE HAWKER FURY II INTERCEPTOR, known also as the Super Fury, equipped No. 25 Squadron in August 1935. It had a more powerful Kestrel engine, wheel spats, a slight increase in wing span and height, and could reach 233m.p.h. at 1,000 ft. But above all it retained the sleek lines of its predecessor and was, without doubt, the most beautiful biplane ever built for the Royal Air Force.

SQN. LDR. FLEMING, seen here leading the Demons of 25 Squadron on their weekly battle climb, was, at this stage in his flying career, a rather disappointed CO. When he swapped his beautiful Furys for the Demons of 41 Squadron at Catterick his first reaction on seeing them was one of disillusionment. They had sagging fabric, evidence of corrosion and oil patches everywhere.

THE AERODROME GATES were flung open to the public in May 1935 for the Empire Air Display, at which Flt. Lts. Clouston and Dainty brought gasps of admiration from over 2,000 spectators when they performed dazzling aerobatics. Clouston waits on the immaculate Hawkinge grass with his Fury I for the signal to take off on his display sequence. In the distance the white-washed hangars and crowds milling around the exhibition can be seen.

THIS AUDAX, 2 Squadron's K3062, made a heavy landing on 9 September 1935, and was struck off charge. A year later, during the Empire Air Day show, when flights of Audax were making a mock attack upon a wood and cardboard fort erected in the middle of the aerodrome, one of them struck a 33,000-volt electricity cable near Holywell. FO Ashton and LAC Simpson died instantly.

ROYAL AIR FORCE
OFFICIAL PROGRAMME

EMPIRE AIR DAY
MAY 29TH 1937

DESPITE THE TRAGEDY OF THE PREVIOUS YEAR aerodrome gates were opened to the public for the annual Air Day in 1937. Spectacular stunt flying brought gasps of admiration from over 4,000 spectators. Smoke bombs were dropped as airmen dressed in white flowing sheets ran amock, shooting off blank cartridges. Timid children ran to their parents as pandemonium reigned over the proceedings.

MEMBERS OF BOTH 2 AND 25 SQUADRONS, with their wives, take a curtain call after their amateur production of *Hawk Island*, staged at the Hawkinge gymnasium in December 1938. From left to right: White, Jeffries, Benito, Mrs Frow, Starr, Mrs Opie, Walford, Mrs Jeffries, Howath, Mrs Chadwell, Green, Mrs Anderson and Peter Stansfeld.

NO. 1 HANGAR IS ON THE RIGHT; the three Officers' Married Quarters are in the centre. The two white patches behind them on the left were the concrete bases for additional O.M.Q's built in 1935. On the extreme right the new officers' mess begins to take shape. Except for No. 1 hangar, all the buildings remain to this day.

THE SUPER FURYS OF 25 SQUADRON line up for refuelling. It will be noticed, I am sure, that the engine cowlings and wheel spats were burnished like chromium. Even though the ground staff took enormous care over and pride in their sleek Furys, droplets of oil often fell on tombstones in the nearby cemetery. Church dignitaries were not amused.

A BLENHEIM LINE-UP, ready for the inspection by No. 25 Squadron's new CO, Sqn. Ldr. J.R. Halling-Pott. Soon after their delivery to Hawkinge four new 12,000 gallon fuel tanks were installed in front of No. 1 hangar. A Court of Enquiry had to be hastily convened to find the culprit who left the control valves open one weekend. Remarkably, no one had thrown a lighted match onto the flooded airfield.

GLOSTER GLADIATORS had equipped 25 Squadron prior to their receiving the Bristol Blenheim 1F, which arrived on 10 December 1938. Conversion training began in earnest in the new year under the eagle eye of the CO, who was still flying a Gladiator in March and April. L1440 sweeps in for a landing over the Gibraltar Lane during the conversion training of pilots. Air gunners were not required to take part at this stage.

THIS HANDLEY PAGE HEYFORD of No. 10 Squadron arrived in May 1937 for the annual Empire Air Display.

THE VILLAGE NEWSAGENT, PERCY PEPIN, delivered newspapers, magazines and headed notepaper to the aerodrome from about 1928 until the aerodrome closed. Pepin ran a mobile shop to the aerodrome on every Empire Air Day display. This picture, taken in 1938, shows a placard of the *Evening Star* which says, '72,000 More Called Up By Mussolini.'

Form 250 (Inset).
(In books of 50)

ROYAL AIR FORCE.

STAFF*
CIVILIAN WORKS* PASS.
TRADING*

No. of Pass................. Holder of Pass _Mr. Dennis Harris_

Address _Stone Lane, Hawkinge_

Occupation _Radar Engineer_

Employer's name _Mr. R. Smith_

Address _87 Joyce Road, Folkestone_

Permission is hereby granted to the Holder of this pass, whose signature appears below, to enter and leave _RAF Station, Hawkinge_ between the hours of _0800_ and _2000_ during the period _All 1939_ to _31/12/39_, for the purpose of conducting the above business.

The Holder of this pass has access to the following :—

....

....

Whether deposit of 2s. 6d. has been paid _No_

Station ....

Date ....19 . Commanding..................................

R.A.F.

Signature of Holder..................................

CONDITIONS ON WHICH PASS IS GRANTED.

1. This pass is issuable only to British subjects.
2. It is not to be issued to those for whom a special Air Ministry Pass is required, vide para. 853, AP 958 (KR & ACI) 1928 Edition.
3. It is not transferable and is to be produced on demand.
4. It does not entitle the holder to enter any part of the establishment unconnected with his business or to remain in the establishment after the expiration of his business. If issued for trading purposes it is available only for the residential portion of the establishment and nowhere else.
5. It is tenable only for the period mentioned, on the expiration of which it is to be surrendered and application made for renewal.
6. The Holder of this pass is forbidden to take photographs or to communicate with the press on service matters.
7. The deposit, if any, of 2s. 6d. on this pass will be forfeited unless the pass is delivered up when required. Application for return of deposit must be accompanied by the receipt.
8. In the event of its loss the Commanding Officer is to be notified immediately.

* Strike out heading not applicable.

[P.T.O.

CIVILIAN WORK PASS.

TAKEN FROM THE COCKPIT of a 2 Squadron Lysander, these photographs by David Kirton show how the aerodrome looked in 1938. Above: the historic Terlingham Manor Farm can be seen on the extreme bottom left and, on the right, No. 6 hangar has been pulled down. Below: this shot reveals the first camouflage attempt with only the hangar roofs completed. The two new O.M.Q.s can be seen middle left (see p. 84), and the completed officers' mess extreme left.

FO B. CHADWELL, station accounts officer, saying goodbye to Mrs Chadwell before he flew to Old Sarum in the Lysander L4704. It was not considered unreasonable in peace-time for wives to be allowed to see their husbands off on these flying trips. While the dark shadows of the German war machine were rolling nearer to England a tighter security system evolved.

THE RAF HAWKINGE CRICKET TEAM pose for the photographer in 1938. They played against teams such as Folkestone, the local newspaper, the *Folkestone Herald*, the Army School of Education, the Harvey Grammar School and many others. They beat the *Herald* team on one occasion by seven wickets. Unfortunately there are no names on the back of this print, but FO B. Chadwell is seated at the centre of the front row.

SECTION FOUR

1940–1942

KNOWN BY THE RAF AS 'BROWN-JOBS', 'E' Company, 6th Buffs Regiment were the first line of defence at the aerodrome in 1940. The majority of soldiers in this group, outside Reindene House on the outskirts of the village, had been called up only about six weeks before this photograph was taken.

THE LYSANDERS OF 2 (A.C.) SQUADRON line up ready for inspection before moving to France on 6 October 1939. Equipment went by road to Dover docks where it was loaded on to ferries. The aircraft flew to Drucat and Abbeville a week later. No. 25 Squadron had moved to Northolt. The hangars now looked forbidding structures; ornamental trees and shrubs had withered beneath the toxic camouflage paint.

FIFTY YEARS ON FROM THE BATTLE OF BRITAIN, Hawkinge is remembered today as the nearest front line fighter station to France, from where the German Air Force unleashed its terror raids. This photograph is one of a series taken at Hawkinge in July 1940 by Fox showing the Hawker Hurricanes of No. 32 Squadron ready to scramble.

THIS RARE POSTER, issued by the Westland Aircraft Company, Yeovil, in 1940, depicts the Army Co-operation squadrons making their Lysander sorties to drop supplies to the beleaguered troops of the BEF at Calais. Air Vice Marshal C.H.B. Blount had organized this operation from Hawkinge under the aegis of Back Component which used the Haskard Target building (see p. 60).

AS A FRONT LINE AIRFIELD, Hawkinge was used continuously for re-arming and refuelling fighter aircraft. Personnel of No. 11 Servicing Flight were to set up a remarkable record of thoroughness and efficiency, dealing with countless fighters which dropped in without warning or ceremony before, during and after combat.

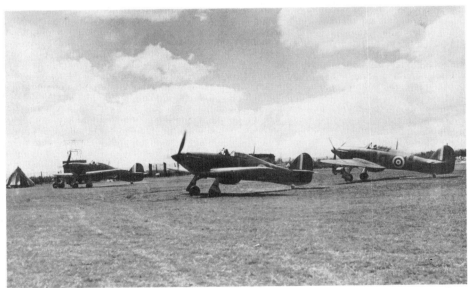

ANOTHER PICTURE IN THE FAMOUS FOX SERIES depicting the Hurricanes of No. 32 Squadron about to scramble from the 'A' Flight dispersal at Hawkinge. Coded GZ-C, the Hurricane N2459, flown by PO D.H. Grice (centre), was shot down in flames on 15 August 1940, south of Harwich. 'Duggie' Grice was rescued from the sea by a Motor Torpedo Boat and admitted to the Royal Navy hospital at Shotley with severe burns.

THE PILOTS OF 32 SQUADRON relax between sorties on the Hawkinge grass in July 1940, with the O.M.Q.s in the background. Left to right: PO R.F. Smythe, PO K.R. Gillman, PO J.E. Procter, Flt. Lt. P.M. Brothers, PO D.H. Grice, PO P.M. Gardner, and PO A.F. Eckford. Of the seven pilots seen here only one did not survive.

ANOTHER FAMOUS PHOTOGRAPH taken at Hawkinge in July 1940 shows the Spitfires of No. 610 (County of Chester) Squadron waiting for the scramble near 'A' Flight dispersal at Gibralter Lane. The Spitfire coded DW-T (P9452) on the extreme right of the print, flown by Peter Lichfield, was shot down off Calais on 18 July 1940. The pilot was presumed killed.

A SPITFIRE OF NO. 66 SQUADRON (X4321) crash-landed beside Barnhurst Lane, Hawkinge the day after a German pilot, Feldwebel Werner Gottschalk, had landed at the aerodrome with his Messerschmitt fighter, unable to make any further progress back to France. The pilot, PO A.W. Bodie, was unhurt and a Special Constable stood guard over the aircraft until it was removed to the aerodrome.

BROKEN PATCHES COVERING THE GUN PORTS in the wings of this Spitfire of 610 Squadron denote the aircraft had been in action and the Browning machine guns fired. Ground crew are seen re-arming the ammunition boxes and clearing the bullet ejection channels. The battery mobile starter is already plugged into its housing ready to start the engine.

IT WAS ALL OVER WITHIN MINUTES. No. 3 hangar lies in ruins after the Luftwaffe air raid on Hawkinge of 12 August 1940. This was the result of Goering's fierce attacks on the south-east of England, intended to soften up our airfields in preparation for Hitler's 'Adler Tag' offensive which was due to start on 13 August 1940.

WHEN HAUPTMANN VON BRAUCHITSCH, leading his Stuka JU87 dive-bombers, was approaching Hawkinge on 15 August 1940 the village barber's shop was full of airmen. An accurate stick of bombs blasted No. 2 hangar and the village streets became alive with hot shrapnel and bullets. Clad only in a bath towel, one young airman rushed out of the barber's shop into the main road. The photograph, by Corporal Troke of the RAF Police, shows No. 2 hangar.

FO 'BOB' HOLLAND gives the 'scramble' over the tannoy system from the little flying control building situated near No. 1 hangar. Hawkinge never possessed the conventional control tower often seen at other airfields. This historic building eventually succumbed to woodworm and decay. It collapsed in gale force winds during the 1970s (see p. 152).

THIS NAAFI MOBILE CANTEEN toured the airfield perimeter and outlying anti-aircraft gun sites within a five-mile radius twice each day. Known to airmen and gunners as the 'tea and wad van', it was often seen in the town of Folkestone supplying tea to members of the Civil Defence personnel during the shelling bombardment of 1943 and '44.

NO. 501 (COUNTY OF GLOUCESTER) SQUADRON scramble from Hawkinge to meet German bomber formations in August 1940. The squadron was to lose six Hurricanes on 16 August. The two seen in this picture were shot down on 18 August 1940. PO K.N.T. Lee baled out, but PO J.W. Bland was killed in SD-T.

PO KEITH R. GILLMAN, photographed at Hawkinge in July 1940, one of the most famous of the Fox photographs. Keith was born in Dover in 1920 and educated at the Dover County School. His picture was widely used in wartime newspapers and magazines and epitomized the youthfulness of the fighter pilots who fought in the Battle of Britain. Keith met his death on 25 August 1940, shot down within sight of his home town.

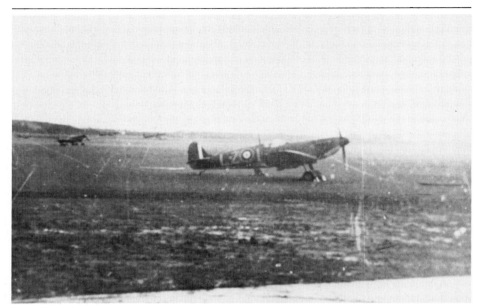

THERE WERE FEW PHOTOGRAPHS TAKEN of No. 421 Flight, formed from their parent squadron No. 66 in October 1940. This one shows Spitfire L-Z-I at Hawkinge in November 1940, the personal mount of CO, Sqn. Ldr. C.P. Green. LZ were the original code letters for No. 66 Squadron and the special flight, formed as a reconnaisance unit, carried the same letters with a stroke between, until they reformed into No. 91 Squadron the following year.

WHEN NO. 421 FLIGHT REFORMED as No. 91 (Nigerian) Squadron on 11 January 1941, they continued to use their Spitfire IIas until receiving the Mark Vs later in the year. Sgt. MacKay's Spitfire IIa was photographed at Hawkinge in early 1941 – serial number P8194 and coded 'M'. Damaged hangars in the background had yet to be pulled down.

GB. 10 99 bc

Hawkinge
Flugplatz

Lft.Kdo. 3   Juli 1941

Länge (östw. Greenw.): 1° 09' 30"   Nördl. Breite: 51° 06' 30"   Zielhöhe über NN 168 m

Karte 1:100000
GB/E Bl. 40 d

Maßstab etwa 1:14 500

GB 10 99 Flugplatz   1 100 x 750 m

1) zerstörte Hallen
2) 1 Werfthalle   etwa   3 400 qm
3) Lagergebäude und
   Werkstätten   etwa   900 qm
4) Unterkunfts- und
   Nebengebäude   etwa   4 000 qm
5) 2 Munitionshäuschen   etwa   50 qm
6) Kleinkampfanlagen

   bebaute Fläche   etwa   8 350 qm

THIS ORIGINAL LUFTWAFFE RECONNAISSANCE PHOTOGRAPH taken in March 1941 shows the aerodrome damaged by bombs, with only No. 1 hangar intact. Creases on the photograph occurred when a soldier found the print at Calais Mark airfield in France, while our troops were advancing through the Pas de Calais in 1944, folded it and put it in his battledress pocket.

FLT. LT. DONALD A.S. MACKAY DFM AND BAR flew as a Sgt. Pilot with No. 501 Squadron in France, before joining No. 421 Flight at Gravesend in October 1940. Don MacKay was awarded his Bar and eventually promoted Flt. Lt. while serving with No. 91 Squadron at Hawkinge. On 15 November 1940, when 421 Flight flew into Hawkinge for the first time, Don MacKay shot down a Dornier 17Z into the sea off Folkestone with a five second burst.

SGT. PILOT DAVID I. KIRTON, who served with No. 2 (A.C.) Squadron at Hawkinge in the late '30s and who was selected for pilot training, joined No. 65 Squadron during the Battle of Britain period. Born in Dover in June 1919, he was shot down near Manston, Isle of Thanet on 8 August 1940 in Spitfire K9911.

THE HAWKINGE VILLAGE NFS TEAM, seen here with their auxiliary pump, was often called to attend fires at the aerodrome. The most notable occasion was when they assisted the local fire brigade and RAF Fire Picket when the aerodrome was bombed on 12 and 15 August 1940. They were especially commended by the A.O.C.-in-C. No. 11 Group Fighter Command.

WHEN NO. 421 FLIGHT BECAME NO. 91 (NIGERIAN) SQUADRON in January 1941 they had been in action continuously since their inception. They had carried out no less than 199 reconnaissance patrols, destroyed 10 enemy aircraft, damaged 9 others and claimed 4 'probables'. This was no mean feat for a handful of dedicated pilots. The photograph shows a line-up of No. 91 Squadron's Mark V Spitfires, which carried two 20mm cannons.

PILOTS OF NO. 91 SQUADRON grouped round a Spitfire Vb, coded DL-H. From left to right: the American Flt. Lt. A.G. 'Art' Donahue, Flt. Lt. R.M.D. 'Sam' Hall, another American Sgt. A.C. Younge, Sgt. R. Ingram, Sgt. F.S. 'Polly' Perkin, Sgt. 'Johnny' Downs, and Sgt. 'Shag' O'Shaugnessy. The squadron was now recognized as a 'Jim Crow' unit.

PILOTS OF THE 'JIM CROW' SQUADRON were of predominantly foreign origin — French, Belgian, Dutch, Norwegian, Canadian, New Zealander or American. This shows the American Sgt. A.C. Younge of Cleveland, USA with his Spitfire Vb, named Cleveland's Challenge. The 20mm cannon of the Mark V Spitfire became a formidable weapon in the hands of these pilots who constantly changed their tactics to confuse the enemy.

THE ACE PILOT SQN. LDR. JEAN DEMOZAY, a Free Frenchman and CO of No. 91 Squadron in 1942, flew under the *nom de guerre* of 'Moses Morlaix', and was awarded the DSO, DFC and Bar, Order of Liberation, Croix de Guerre with nine palms. His final score of enemy aircraft shot down totalled twenty-one. He was tragically killed on 19 December 1945, in a jet.

SGT. 'JOHNNY' DOWNS OF 91 SQUADRON is being debriefed by the squadron 'spy' (Intelligence Officer) after returning from a reconnaissance patrol in 1942. Reconnaissance patrols were usually operated by two Spitfires, one going from Dieppe to Cap Gris Nez on the westward route while the other went from Ostend to Cap Gris Nez on the eastward route. They were known by the local civilians as the 'Gert and Daisy' patrol.

THE SOUTH AFRICAN PILOT FLT. LT. J.J. LE ROUX DFC, of 91 Squadron, showing the Springbok emblem on his Mae West inflatable jacket. Jacobus Le Roux was later credited with shooting-up the German staff car in which the German General Rommel was a passenger. Later, as a Sqn. Ldr., Le Roux was credited with twenty-three enemy aircraft destroyed and had received three Bars to his DFC. He was killed on 19 September 1944.

FLT. LT. R.M.D. HALL DFC, of 91 Squadron, had volunteered to become a fighter pilot before the Battle of Britain period. When 'Art' Donahue went 'missing' over the Ostend area in 1942 Roger Hall was sent to look for him. Off Cap Gris Nez visibility was down to below 200 ft. Roger was in a typical pea-souper. Searching for Donahue was out of the question. Roger flew back to Hawkinge by his instruments and had to be talked down to a landing. 'Art' Donahue was never found.

WHEN A *KENT MESSENGER* PHOTOGRAPHER walked into the officers' mess one lunch-time he netted this group. Among them is the station chaplain, the medical officer, the anti-aircraft liaison officer known as 'Guns', a couple of intelligence officers, nine pilots and an American liaison officer.

SQN. LDR. DEMOZAY INSISTED that 'B' Flight ground crew should have their photo taken too. The 'Erks' were as enthusiastic as the pilots. Combat reports were often discussed well into the night and great rivalry existed between 'A' and 'B' Flights. Spitfires were fussed over into the late hours, and woe betide any pilot who had forgotten to activate his camera button, or left his flaps in the 'locked-down' position, or left the gun-button safety catch in the 'off' position.

A SPITFIRE Vb STANDS AS A BACKCLOTH to this group of 91 Squadron pilots. Flt. Lt. Geoff Pannell, a New Zealander, stands cap-less on the extreme left, and next to him, leaning on the propeller blade, is Sqn. Ldr. Demozay. Of the nine pilots in this photograph, four have the DFC. The two pilots on the right, with gaiters, are ready for their 'Gert and Daisy' dusk patrol.

LT. WERNER SCHLATHER, of II/LGII, operating from the Calais Mark airfield on the French coast, decided to make a single-handed lightning attack on Hawkinge on 8 February 1941. His Messerschmitt Bf 109 was hit by the Hawkinge gunners while Schlather was completing a loop over the airfield. His body was recovered from a 20ft crater near Arpinge.

THE 'JIM CROW' SQUADRON were destined to become one of the most professional fighter-reconnaissance squadrons in Fighter Command. This was largely due to the pilots developing their own system of navigation, and their incredible audacity in attacking the enemy at close quarters and in every conceivable situation. Sgt 'Johnny' Down sits above his fellow pilots who are grouped around his Mark V Spitfire.

FIGHTER SQUADRONS in 1942 had begun to take the initiative and to some extent gain a foothold in air superiority. Pilots scoured the French coast looking for trouble, often shooting-up German airfields in an attempt to stir up a hornets' nest. It was on one of these coastal sweeps that 'Johnny' Down was very nearly shot down. This shows the damaged elevator of Down's Spitfire.

THE 'JIM CROW' PILOTS were without exception eager to cross swords with the Luftwaffe, and they sometimes flew at full squadron strength. New Zealander Geoff Pannell DFC stands on the left of this foursome near the 'A' Flight dispersal, Gibraltar Lane.

CANADIAN SGT. 'BILL' SYKES sits in the cockpit of his Spitfire AR370. He was reported missing over Dieppe on 15 June 1942. On 20 April 1941 he had 'ditched' in the sea about 400 yd off Sandgate when he ran out of fuel. He swam ashore on that occasion. Previously he had flown so close to the sea that three inches had been knocked off his propeller blades! His ground crew fined him five shillings.

THIS SPITFIRE IIa BELONGING TO 421 FLIGHT, previously coded L-Z-I, became DL-I when the Flight formed 91 Squadron. Originally flown by the 421 CO, Sqn. Ldr. C.P. Green, it is flown here in early 1941 by Sgt. 'Johnny' Down.

FLT. SGT. SAM HONNOR, seen here standing in the cockpit of a 91 Squadron Spitfire, was mentioned in despatches for services to the squadron. His skill in patching-up damaged aircraft was said to be no less than outstanding. Bad weather conditions usually grounded most other fighter squadrons, but the 'Jim Crow' unit used the low cloud cover and intermittent rain squalls to fly on their special missions.

PO W. 'BILLY' ORR went missing on a reconnaissance sortie over Dieppe on 22 July 1942 in Spitfire BL816. Alone, and taking photographs for the forthcoming Operation Jubilee, the Dieppe raid of 19 August 1942, 'Billy' may have become disorientated in swirling sea mists.

THIS AERIAL PHOTOGRAPH, taken in the 1960s by Skyfotos Ltd, shows the hard-standings of hangars Nos 2 and 3 which were demolished by the air raids of 1940.

THIS UNOFFICIAL INSIGNIA OF NO. 277 (A.S.R.) (AIR SEA RESCUE) SQUADRON was designed and painted by Sgt. D. Hartwell. As a large mural in full colour it adorned the wall of the crew room. The room was taken over by the WAAF and used as a lecture room in the late 1940s and the mural was painted over.

THE FIRST A.S.R. LYSANDER TO OPERATE FROM HAWKINGE was borrowed from 'B' Flight, No. 4 Army Co-operation Squadron, then at Manston, and began searching sorties in December 1940. This is the only known photograph of that first Lysander, with its two Hurricane escorts, sitting on the grass near Aerodrome Road.

ONE OF THE FINEST PHOTOGRAPHS OF A 277 SQUADRON LYSANDER AT HAWKINGE was taken when the *Kent Messenger* team arrived in 1942. Flt. Lt. 'Jackie' Spence, a Canadian, sits in the cockpit while an M8 inflatable dinghy is stowed away in the wheel flap cradle.

ANOTHER CANADIAN serving in 277 Squadron was FO Roy Kipping, seen here in the cockpit of his Spitfire (A.S.R.) Vb. The A.S.R. Spitfire had clipped wings which allowed greater manoeuvrability at very low level whilst the pilot searched for 'ditched' airmen in the sea. This photograph was taken by the Canadian Press who visited RAF stations where Canadians were in action.

SGT. D. WADDINGTON, another 277 Squadron pilot, flew the Lysanders and the Walrus amphibians during many of the hazardous rescue missions operated over the English Channel and the North Sea. Here he sits on his motorbike outside the A.S.R. crew room. The building, formerly the photographic section, remains to this day, used now by the Hawkinge parish council.

THIS 30 FT DIAMETER BOWL MIRROR, erected on the Downs above Hythe in the 1930s, remains *in situ* today, with its skeletal sound locator and underground listener's post. Fears that Germany would find a way to jam our radar system in 1943 led to emergency experiments carried out by Post Office engineers. A range of fifty miles was achieved, but this method of enemy aircraft detection was never used and it was abandoned.

PRESURE ON EXISTING A.S.R. UNITS persuaded the Air Ministry to review the much-maligned Boulton Paul Defiant. By May 1942 No. 277 (A.S.R.) Squadron had received six of them to supplement the four Lysanders on strength. But once again the Defiant proved considerably less then spectacular and within six months had been replaced by the clipped-wing Spitfire Vb. This shows a 277 Squadron Defiant with red code letters BA-A.

SGT. JACKIE ROSE, seated behind his twin .5 Browning machine-gun in the rear cockpit of an A.S.R. Lysander, prepares for a long vigil over the grey wastes of the English Channel. Born in Derby, Sgt. Rose used to sing in harmony with his pilot Roy Kipping, while they searched for 'ditched' air crew. Stooging along at 130 m.p.h. the lone Lysander was easy prey for a vigilant German fighter pilot.

SECTION FIVE

1943–1944

SQN. LDR. 'JACKIE' SPENCE (centre) AND SGT. DONALD WADDINGTON (on the left), with a couple of other 277 Squadron pilots, run out of the crew room at Hawkinge to their aircraft sitting on the grass only a few yards away. They had done this hundreds of times, for real, when Group had signalled a 'customer' in the drink at this or that map reference.

ONE OF THE SUPERMARINE WALRUS AMPHIBIANS used by 'B' Flight, 277 (A.S.R.) Squadron at Hawkinge from about 1942 to 1944. Coded BA-D, with the serial number HD908, this particular Walrus II had been built by the Saunders Roe Company for the Royal Navy, and was then transferred to the RAF for air sea rescue duties.

THE CANADIAN PILOT 'JACKIE' SPENCE, flying with 277 Squadron at Hawkinge, was photographed here when he was a Flight Lieutenant. Later promoted to Sqn. Ldr., he received the DFC, and was shot-up in a Defiant by a Focke-Wulf 190 over the Channel when his gunner informed him that the .5 Brownings had jammed! Fortunately, the FW 190 was apparently out of cannon shells and aborted his attack. Survival in war is a matter of luck — sometimes!

SGT. 'STICKER' GLEW was an air-gunner with 277 Squadron. He and his wife rented accommodation in Shorncliffe Road, Folkestone while he served at Hawkinge. Unfortunately, 'Sticker' was to lose his life while flying in Malta, later in the war.

PILOTS, AIRCREW AND GROUNDCREW OF 'B' FLIGHT, 277 SQUADRON at Hawkinge in 1943. The record of the A.S.R. unit at the airfield is quite remarkable. It is one of courage and endurance and, perhaps above all, it reveals a commendable sense of responsibility towards saving human lives.

NO. 277 SQUADRON MEMBERS pose for an amateur camera shot while off-duty from the rigours of air sea searches. It is hard to imagine these men, in the most appalling weather conditions, searching hour after hour over the English Channel and North Sea, looking for a minute shape on the grey wastes.

FLT. LT. DOUG HARTWELL got his Lysander off the ground despite the gale force winds on 16 April 1942. Climbing over Reindene Wood near Swingfield, the big Mercury engine suddenly stopped. Losing height rapidly, the Lysander's undercarriage caught the tree tops, and the aircraft flipped over into a field. Although Hartwell had been pinned to his seat by the engine thrusting backwards he managed to claw his way out of the wreckage and dragged his gunner, Sgt. G.W. Jones, to safety. Sgt. Jones was seriously injured and never flew again.

ALONE IN HIS DINGHY for a day or for just an hour, a 'ditched' pilot, seeing an A.S.R. Lysander circling overhead, would have experienced great relief. The twenty-four hour ordeal of PO Turek of No. 609 Squadron would fill a page. Turek was about ten miles from the mouth of the Somme estuary when he was finally rescued by a Walrus from under the very noses of the Germans. Soaked to the skin, Turek was hauled aboard. PO Standen was unable to get the Walrus to take off from the heavy seas. They were eventually towed into Dover harbour by an RAF launch.

RE-ARMING THE .5 BROWNING MACHINE-GUNS of a Lysander was always the responsibility of the air-gunner who flew in the machine. New Zealander Sgt. Johnny Snell is in the cockpit feeding-in the ammunition belts to his twin Brownings.

THE RESPONSIBILITY for seeing that the M8 rubber dinghy was fitted correctly on the wheel spats was the pilot's. Canadian pilot 'Jackie' Spence stands, back to the Lysander, while Sgt. Snell looks on from the right.

THE FIRST AMERICAN EAGLE SQUADRON in Fighter Command became operational in August 1941. This Spitfire IIa of No. 71 Eagle Squadron, coded XR-D (P7308), on a cross-Channel sortie on 27 August, made an emergency landing at Hawkinge with rear fuselage damage.

AMERICAN 'ART' DONAHUE, who had seen action in 1940, had volunteered for the Far East in 1941 and became Flight Commander with No. 258 Squadron, flying Hurricanes in the defence of Ceylon. He was one of the last to leave Singapore when the Japanese invaded Malaya. Back with 91 Squadron in 1942, he just disappeared from the radar screen on 11 September when tracking an elusive JU88 night-fighter. He is seen here in the centre of this trio at Hawkinge.

SGT. D.R. HARTWELL, Lysander pilot of the resident Air Sea Rescue squadron, took off from the airfield on the evening of 16 April 1942. The Mercury engine developed a fault soon after take off and the Lysander crashed beside Reindene Wood (see p. 124).

FLT. LT. 'TUG' WILSON, RAAF, flew the Supermarine Walrus on air sea rescue sorties from Hawkinge with 277 Squadron.

SQN. LDR. BARON M.G.L. DONNET DFC WITH FLT. SGT. GEBREUCQ of 'B' Flight, No. 350 (Belgium) Squadron. As Wing Commander (Flying), 'Mike' Donnet (later Lt.-General Aviateur, CVO, DFC, Nato) led the Hawkinge Wing in August 1944. His book *Flight to Freedom* outlined his courageous escape from Brussels in July 1941, in an SV4 Stampe biplane.

FO MICHAEL BENTINE, Intelligence Officer to No. 350 (Belgium) Squadron, is now better known as an artist, author and comedian. He is seen here at Hawkinge in 1944 painting a Red Indian motif on the CO's Spitfire. Squadron personnel were mostly Belgian nationals, many of whom had escaped from their own country. No. 350 pilots distinguished themselves during the Dieppe raid when they destroyed seven enemy aircraft.

THERE HAD BEEN MANY DRAMATIC CRASHES on the airfield by 1943, and each had its own peculiar characteristics. This Flying Fortress B17, believed to have been from the 305th Bomber Group G of USAAF, crash-landed at Hawkinge on 15 September 1943 and very nearly toppled over the airfield boundary on to Terlingham Manor Farm.

THE 'JIM CROW' SQUADRON were to re-equip with the new Spitfire Mk XII. They were relieved by No. 41 Squadron. A Spitfire Mk XII of No. 41 Squadron shows off its paces as well as the twin cannon (20mm), the clipped wing tips and pointed fin. The Rolls-Royce Merlin engine had been replaced by the Griffin.

LT.-COL. CHESLEY G. PETERSON DSO, DSC, DFC, US AIR MEDAL AND PURPLE HEART, was Tactical Operations Officer 8th USAAF Fighter Command at 23 years of age. A veteran of the Eagle Squadron (RAF), he was the most decorated man in the USAAF in England when this photograph was taken at Gravesend on 3 September 1943. Peterson had twice been rescued from the English Channel by No. 277 Squadron. Wg/Cdr. R.C. Wilkinson DFM and Bar, OBE, CO of Gravesend, stands on his left, and his wife and Wg/Cdr A. Linney OBE, CO of No. 277 Squadron, on his right. On behalf of the USAAF, Peterson presented a cheque for £100 to the comforts fund of the A.S.R. unit. He received a model of a Walrus in return.

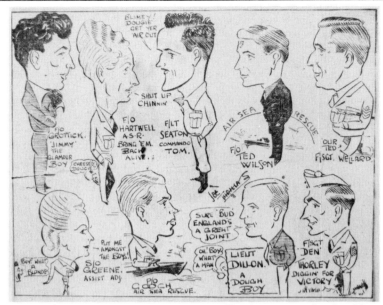

'FLASHES FROM AN AIR STATION IN THE SOUTH EAST.' These cartoons, by Joe Thomas, were published in the *Kent Messenger* newspaper in 1943 and 1944. Joe Thomas expertly caught the station personalities of the time.

SOME MORE HAWKINGE PERSONALITIES from the sketch pad of Joe Thomas.

PILOTS OF THE 'JIM CROW' SQUADRON in their Mae Wests stand round Annie's tea and wad van in 1942. From left to right: PO 'Demo' De Moline (Free French), PO Ingram, PO Edwards, PO Heap, PO Lambert (alias Copeland, Free French), and 'Scotty' Downer. Of the seven pilots shown here five were to lose their lives.

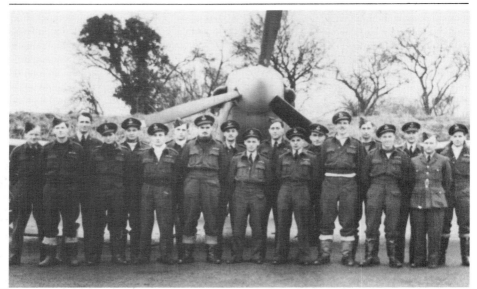

SQN. LDR. R.H. HARRIES DFC is seen here in the centre of this 91 Squadron photograph, taken in December 1942. Already a well-known personality, Harries, now CO, was eventually to total twenty-one victories. Harries and his pilots became local heroes on 25 May 1943, when they shot down five FW 190s over Folkestone without loss to the squadron.

MEMBERS OF NO. 855 FLEET AIR ARM SQUADRON relax at the Black Horse inn, Densole. No. 855 Squadron arrived at Hawkinge on 23 May 1944, and No. 854 arrived a week later. Both squadrons, flying the TBF1 Grumman Avenger, were soon to operate Channel sweeps prior to 'Operation Overlord', the Normandy invasion on 6 June 1944.

MR AND MRS TUNBRIDGE, licensees of the Black Horse, are seen here with pilots and observers at the annex where regular dances were held. Channel patrols before, during and after D-Day were succinctly described as 'Channel Stop'.

THE TBF1 AVENGERS had no trouble operating out of Hawkinge in spite of their ponderous appearance. One major 'flap' occurred when JZ434, coded 5L, failed to take off at 0830hrs on 5 June 1944. Sub-Lt. Peter Litherland was at the controls, with Sub-Lt. Ken Belch as observer and Sub-Lt. Charles Porter as air-gunner/bomb-aimer.

THE AVENGER skimmed over a machine-gun emplacement and ploughed through barbed-wire entanglements on its belly. Litherland and Belch pulled the air-gunner clear. They fell at the feet of a crowd of airmen who beat a hasty retreat when they were informed there was a 2,000 lb bomb load still intact in the fuselage.

SUB-LT. ROGER JOHNSON took off from Hawkinge at fifteen minutes before midnight on the night of 22/23 July 1944, for a patrol from Cap Gris Nez to Cap d'Antifer and back. Roger depicts here the accurate firepower of an E-boat flotilla, which turned his Avenger into a fireball. After being in the water for over twenty-four hours he was eventually picked up by a German patrol boat off Dieppe. He was sent to Stalag Luft III; and only returned to Hawkinge forty years later!

SECTION SIX

1945–1961

DAME FELICITY HANBURY, then Director of WAAF, is seen here in the cab of a 'Battle of Britain' class locomotive, after the naming ceremony at Dover Priory station on 25 June 1948, when the locomotive was named *Hawkinge*.

THE WAAF TECHNICAL TRAINING UNIT AT HAWKINGE provided the Guard of Honour at Dover Priory station for the naming ceremony of the locomotive. When the locomotive was eventually scrapped one name plate was held at the Elham Rural District Council offices at Lyminge, while the other was on display at the Harvey Grammar School, Folkestone.

SUCCESSFUL WAAF CANDIDATES perform a march past after completing their training courses in drill and administration duties with the WAAF Technical Training Unit. Successful NCOs found themselves posted to Recruit Training Centres in various parts of the British Isles.

ONE OF THE SEVERAL NCO'S COURSES at Hawkinge. The WAAF Technical Training Centre began here in July 1947. Under the command of Group Officer N. Dinnie, refresher courses involved many hundreds of women who were subjected to drill, drill and more drill. Their presence brought a new lease of life to the old aerodrome, however.

HER MAJESTY QUEEN ELIZABETH, now the Queen Mother, talks to Dame Henrietta Barnett OBE, (WAAF), Group Officer Commanding, during the royal visit to Hawkinge in 1952. Marshal of the Royal Air Force, Sir William Dickson GCB, KBE, DSO, AFC, the first Station Commander at Hawkinge in 1935, stands to the right of the Queen Mother.

GROUP OFFICER F.B. HILL (centre) enjoying Dame Henrietta Barnett's attempts to toss a pancake in the Hawkinge kitchen.

THE DUCHESS OF GLOUCESTER, accompanied by Air Commandant Dame Jean Bromet (formerly Jean Conan Doyle, daughter of the famous novelist, Sir Arthur Conan Doyle), during a visit to Hawkinge in 1952, to inspect the Women's Royal Air Force Officer Course Training Unit Depot. The WRAF courses, originally of three months duration, had been extended to six months by early 1961. The young ladies were drawn from a cross-section of society.

IN THE HAWKINGE OFFICERS' MESS ANTE-ROOM are, from left to right: Air Marshal Sir Walter Kyle, Air Commodore Anne Stephens (Director of WRAF), Marshal of the Royal Air Force, Sir William Dickson, Wing Officer Benson (CO of WRAF Depot), Air Commandant Jean Bromet, Air Vice Marshal Checksfield, Group Officer F.B. Hill, -?-.

THIS SPITFIRE IX, serial number MK356, was the station gate guardian from late 1944 until the aerodrome closed in December 1961. It had served with No. 443 squadron and flown over the D-Day landings. Its ignominious 'wheels up' landing at Ford, on 13 June 1944, may have been fortuitous as it provided Hawkinge with its one and only gate guardian.

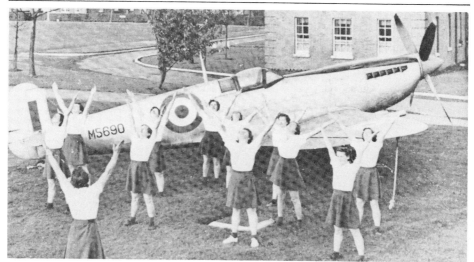

THE HAWKINGE GATE GUARDIAN MK356 was renumbered M5690, making it a non-flying instructional airframe. The correct number should have been 5690M. The WRAFs performing their physical jerks at the WRAF O.C.T.U. had their minds on other things, however.

MAYPOLE COTTAGE in Hawkinge village was requisitioned by the Air Ministry as, indeed, were many other properties. The cottage was used by the 'Y' Service, where WAAF telegraphists listened-in to German wireless transmissions from 1940 onwards. Soldiers guarding the cottage throughout the last war left behind their service numbers, names, ranks and even home addresses, scratched on the leaded windows.

FO SCOTT-FARNIE began the first 'Y' Service post at RAF Hawkinge in February 1940. Listening-in to German radio traffic was part of the intelligence network and many listening posts were set up throughout the country. German-speaking WAAFs were the first translators and they maintained a twenty-four hour watch system. WAAFs and airmen of the 'Y' Service are photographed here at Capel le Ferne, near the cliffs above Folkestone.

THE HOME GLIDING SCHOOL came to Hawkinge between 1955 and 1960, and local ATC squadrons took advantage of this facility. In 1956 a young ATC cadet under gliding instruction had a narrow escape when he landed on the roof of 'Ditchling', the home and business premises of Eric Haddow, the village hairdresser.

THERE ARE NOT MANY VILLAGES IN THE BRITISH ISLES which can boast having a 'Battle of Britain' class locomotive named after it. *Hawkinge* hauled passenger services on most of the Southern Region's railway network until it was scrapped in 1960. One of the tragedies is that the engine was never recovered from the breaker's yard before it was cut up.

THE HAWKINGE GATE GUARDIAN, Spitfire Mk IX (MK356), leaves the aerodrome for RAF Locking in 1961. It went under protest from the then Folkestone Borough Council who wanted it displayed on the Leas. It did return briefly in June 1968, during the filming of the epic film *The Battle of Britain*.

HOCKLY SOLE, a mock-Elizabethan half-timbered house in the Alkham Valley, once the home of Sir Herbert and Lady Raphael, was taken over by the Air Ministry under the Emergency Powers Act, and was known as Hawkinge 'D'. Although originally requisitioned for tired fighter pilots, its real function has never been established.

BUILT IN 1917 AS PART OF THE ORIGINAL BUILDING PROGRAMME, these prefabricated huts, used by the Royal Flying Corps, remained in constant use throughout the airfield's history. They were demolished in the late 1960s.

THESE WOODEN HUTS were erected during the Second World War after half of the barracks block accommodation received bomb damage during 1940 and 1941. Ground staff were billeted in them as well as the RAF Regiment when they arrived for airfield defence. When the Canadian squadrons came in 1944 personnel displayed boards outside them which said 'Lazy Y Ranch'. Later still, the huts were to house WAAFs on their NCO courses. One or two are still used in the village today.

THE AIRMEN'S NAAFI, built in the late 1920s, still stands, converted into flats for local families. During the 1950s airmen made themselves unpopular with WAAF instructors when they held nightly sing-songs in the NAAFI round a beer-soaked piano. They provided the young O.C.T.U. girls with a congenial, if somewhat bawdy insight into service life!

ONE OF TWO BARRACK BLOCKS built in the 1930s to the regular RAF pattern. Although now converted into flats they still, outwardly, retain their original design. During the bombing raids of 1940 and 1941, much of the roof was demolished and the blocks became uninhabitable.

THIS SORRY-LOOKING BUILDING, photographed in 1970 by the author, was once the sports pavilion. It held the flares and rubber dinghies for the Air Sea Rescue squadron during the last war, and had survived the bombing raids and strafing attacks of the Messerschmitt fighter-bombers. It finally succumbed to a force eight gale.

THE TINY MORTUARY, the last resting place before burial of many courageous pilots, both English and German, was finally demolished in 1986. It had remained boarded up for many years, its future uncertain.

MAIN ENTRANCE AND GUARD ROOM, R.A.F. STATION, HAWKINGE.   2

THIS SHOESMITH & ETHERIDGE POSTCARD captures the atmosphere of Hawkinge when it had become the home for the WAAF Technical Training Unit in 1947. The Spitfire gate guardian can be seen under the trees on the left of the picture.

THE WATER TOWER, built during the First World War, remained standing until the late 1970s. It had been holed by German bomb fragments and shell shrapnel but stood throughout the last war. A housing estate has since been built on the site and covers almost the whole of the camp area.

EX-SGT. 'PADDY' CLARE, who had served at RAF Hawkinge, takes a nostalgic last look round the old airfield in the late 1960s. Soon after this photograph was taken the large board fell down and lay decaying for many years afterwards.

THE SERGEANTS' MESS in 1976. Part of it had been demolished during an air raid and later rebuilt to the original specifications.

THE MAIN ENTRANCE TO RAF HAWKINGE in 1976. The guard room on the right and fire station on the left stand, quietly decaying, in the autumn sunshine; the board has fallen from its frame.

THE LITTLE FLYING CONTROL ROOM, desperately hanging on to the memories of yesteryear (see p. 99). Gale force winds howled through the fragile structure until, unable to withstand a force eight, it finally collapsed.

THE CHURCH OF ST HUGH OF LINCOLN was erected on the site of the original parachute bay and almost opposite the Bijou Cottage. The parachute bay had been partitioned off to accommodate services in the last war.

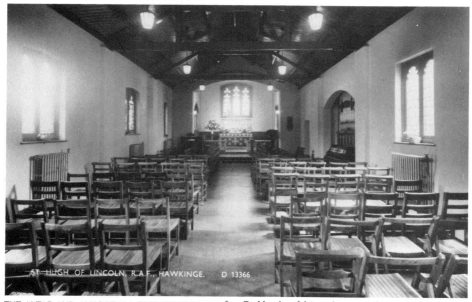

THE ALTAR AND ALMOST ALL THE FURNISHINGS for St Hugh of Lincoln, were brought from the chapel of Sherwood Lodge, Nottingham, where they had been previously associated with No. 504 (County of Nottingham) Squadron.

AMERICAN FILM DIRECTOR HARRY SALZMAN arrived at Hawkinge in June 1968 to shoot the film sequence for that epic film *The Battle of Britain*. This static Spitfire, a non-runner and unable to fly, stood proudly on the grass in its sandbagged mock dispersal. It bore the fictitious code letters of an imaginary squadron.

THE PINEWOOD STUDIO TECHNICIANS built this huge, mock hangar at Hawkinge. The intention was to blow it up during a sequence to simulate an aerodrome being bombed, but Hawkinge parish council objected. The sequence was shot at Duxford where an original pattern Belfast hangar was destroyed.

FROM THE SKETCH PAD OF CAPTAIN BRIAN C. SHERRAN, Royal Engineers, who had been stationed at Hawkinge in 1944, we see a Liberator of the USAAF with one engine knocked out, which nose-dived in the middle of the airfield on 1 March 1944.

THIS B17 FLYING FORTRESS, 42-30849, operated from Podington with the 325th Bomber Squadron, USAAF, 92nd Bomber Group. Carrying the nose-art 'Fart Sack', it crashed at Hawkinge after making a raid on Gristmont and Reims on 1 May 1944. It had been escorted, severely damaged, by an A.S.R. Spitfire.

THIS USAAF MARAUDER belly-flopped on to the airfield after attacking V1 launching sites in the Pas de Calais on 26 June 1944.

BRIAN SHERRAN CAPTURES THE MOMENT when the Marauder, repaired and good as new, takes off from Hawkinge on 13 July 1944, just nineteen days after it made a crash-landing.

THIS DRAWING OF THE CRASHED TBF1 AVENGER (5L) of No. 855 Squadron Fleet Air Arm was, for many years, the only visual evidence recorded, until photographs were found in Canada. (See pp. 135 and 136).

R.A.F. PARADE GROUND, HAWKINGE. 1451.

SHOESMITH & ETHERIDGE POSTCARDS were sold at the village newsagents in Hawkinge for many years. This one, in the aerodrome series, shows the parade ground where Warrant Officers and drill instructors exercised their unique authority over airmen and WAAFs. A barrack block is on the left and the NAAFI is on the far side of the parade ground.

PETER GILES, author, artist and professional singer, visited the aerodrome with his sketch pad in 1982. He was just in time to catch the mood of the decaying buildings before some of them were demolished, making space for the new, modern housing estate which now covers the camp site. Peter's sketches are a sad reminder that history was made here, and that in every corner of the aerodrome memories lurk, only to be revived by the sensitive mind.

THE LAST POST was sounded at dusk on Friday 8 December 1961 as the RAF ensign slowly descended for the last time and the aerodrome finally closed down. This slab of concrete, upon which were inscribed the names of pilots of 'B' Flight, No. 91 Squadron, disappeared without trace. It is believed it was whisked away into the darkness, like the many eminent guests who attended the close-down ceremony on that cold and bleak day in 1961.

A MEMORIAL now stands on a small plot in front of the former gymnasium, the result of the author's personal efforts. It is dedicated to all those who served at RAF Hawkinge. Marshal of the Royal Air Force, Sir William F. Dickson GCB, KBE, DSO, AFC stands with the author after the unveiling of the memorial on 29 April 1978. An inscription on the bronze tablet reads:
HISTORY WITH ITS FLICKERING LAMP STUMBLES ALONG THE TRAIL OF THE PAST, TRYING TO RECONSTRUCT ITS SCENES, TO REVIVE ITS ECHOES, AND REKINDLE WITH PALE GLEAMS THE PASSION OF FORMER YEARS (from a speech made in the House of Commons on 12 November 1940, by Winston S. Churchill).

ACKNOWLEDGEMENTS

I acknowledge with deep gratitude the contributions made by those who, over the past twenty years, generously allowed me the use of photographs from their personal collections.

His Grace the Duke of Hamilton PC KT GCVO AFC
Beisiegel, W.K., OBE, Air Commodore
Geddes, A.J.W., CBE, DSO, Air Commodore
Probyn, H.M., CB, CBE, DSO, Air Commodore
Clappen, D.W., CB, Air Commodore
Stansfeld, P.W., CBE, DFC, Group Captain • Ford, R.J.A., CBE, Group Captain
Stewart, C., CBE, DSO, AFC, Group Captain
Beamish, C.E. St J., DFC, Group Captain
Williams, D.M.W., (WRAF) Group Captain
Bromet, J., (WRAF) Air Commandant, Dame
Upton, D.A., OBE, Wing Commander
Swann, W.E., Wing Commander • Fleming, D.M., Wing Commander
Landry, F., AFC, Wing Commander • Jeffery, W.T., AFC, Squadron Leader
Kerchey, F., Squadron Leader • McKay, G.R.S., DFC, Squadron Leader
Hall, R.M.D., DFC, Flight Lieutenant • Burke, P.L., DFC, AFC, Flight Lieutenant
Hartwell, D.R., Flight Lieutenant • Waddington, D., Warrant Officer
Pritchard, Dr Stephen • Kettle, E • Down, J.K., Flight Lieutenant • Haddow, E.
Cook, R. • Gulvin, S.G. • Marwood, R. • Mynard, C.
Manuel, W.L. • Newman, S.M. • Belch, K. (F.A.A.) • Weeks, L.H.
Kipping, R., Flight Lieutenant • Wiseman-Clarke, F.W., Group Captain
Pepin, P. • Puttee, R.E. • Sherran, B.C. • Chadwell, R. • Russell, A.V.
Kirton, V. • Johnson, R. (F.A.A.) • Bass, C.J. • Tunbridge, P.
Elliot, C.